Dorothy Richardson

DOROTHY RICHARDSON

by CAESAR R. BLAKE

FOREWORD BY LESLIE FIEDLER

THE UNIVERSITY OF MICHIGAN PRESS

ANN ARBOR

ACKNOWLEDGMENT is made of a grant for publication of this book from the Horace H. Rackham School of Graduate Studies, The University of Michigan.

Manufactured in the United States of America by
The Haddon Craftsmen, Inc., Scranton, Pennsylvania

FOR MY PARENTS

Bishop and Mrs. Walter W. Slade

Foreword

BY LESLIE FIEDLER

It is with the *dulness* of Dorothy Richardson that we must begin; for it is that dulness which made her once, in Ford Madox Ford's phrase, "the most abominably unknown contemporary writer"; and it is that dulness which keeps her now, though better known, the most abominably unread recent novelist.

The common reader can begin by understanding at least the peculiar nature of the dulness which characterizes Miss Richardson's 2,000 page novel, called in its final recension *Pilgrimage:* not really as long a book, the author kept reassuring her recalcitrant public, as it seemed when it was originally published in twelve volumes over more than twenty years. And, indeed, *Pilgrimage* is not quite so monstrous as the pregnancy which produced it; but even reduced to four thickish volumes in the edition of 1938 (the first volume appeared in 1915) it is not noticeably short. Yet it must be said that its special dulness is not a function of its length; all fat, ambitious novels have their *longeurs,* Balzac's and Proust's and Tolstoy's, as well as the *Clarissa* of the first Richardson with whom the form began. It is essential to the novel that it aspire to fatness and ambition; and the boredom it creates is one source of its authority, a warranty of its commitment to truth and the dull reality we all inhabit. Yet the ennui generated by Miss Richardson is different in kind from, say, that produced by Melville in the cetological chapters of *Moby Dick*.

Hers is, however, no more the accidental dulness of imprecision and incoherence than it is the generic dulness without which we would scarcely recognize a novel. The boredom we feel before we have finished Henry Miller's *Tropic of Capricorn* or Thomas Wolfe's *The Web and the Rock* or M. G. Lewis's *The Monk* is an embarrassed boredom before the overemphatic assertion of feelings which we cannot share because they are never fictionally proved. Such excess and sentimentality are, of course, utterly alien to Miss Richardson; and yet she is not the kind of fictionist who considers merely having escaped them a sufficient proof of his artistic virtue. Her systematic de-emphasis differs radically from the sweetly reasonable monotone of such pseudo-novelists as William Dean Howells, James Cozzens, J. P. Marquand, or C. P. Snow, who seem to stake their whole claim on *not* being Dostoevsky, i.e., not being hysterical, disturbing, extreme or more than moderately exciting. Such de-caffeinated fiction—guaranteed to keep no one awake—is an *ersatz* of literature manufactured by complacent (or reasonably troubled) middlebrows for the consumption of other middlebrows, who might otherwise not be complacent (or reasonably troubled) enough.

Miss Richardson's long novel is, however, neither reasonable or philistine; it is unequivocally experimental, *avant-garde* in a way perhaps no longer possible. It belongs, that is to say, to that dazzlingly offensive cluster of novels produced in the first decades of our century by writers like Proust, Joyce, Virginia Woolf, and William Faulkner; a kind of book anticipated by Henry James in its desire to make not experience but the experiencing mind the center of fiction, and to make form a function of sensibility. Only after her lifework had been completed, did Miss Richardson realize that she and her contemporaries were, in fact, attempting to *restore* to the novel an awareness of its original function. In the Foreword to the 1938 edition of *Pilgrimage,* she quotes a passage from Goethe in which he asserts that "the thought processes of the principal figure" must .be the chief concern of the novel; but she does not pause to note that Goethe's examples come from *Grandison, Pamela,* and *Clarissa,* the immensely long fiction of Samuel Richardson of whom it was observed (as it might well have been of his namesake) that anyone reading him for the story might as well hang himself!

It is the fate of Dorothy Richardson to be quite as baffling and unorthodox as any of her more flamboyant opposite numbers but to be so palely, *dully.* Hers is the least acceptable of dulnesses, the sort of *avant-garde* dulness inevitable once one has abandoned the expected delights attendant on the fully articulated plot: the suspense, the reversal and recognition—and has refused to replace them either with the "witty exploitation of ideas" (Miss Richardson uses the phrase of James and Conrad, but it would serve equally well for Joyce or Proust) or the sensitive exploitation of nuances (as in Mrs. Woolf).

Not only at the end of *Ulysses* but also at the close of *Finnegans Wake,* Joyce has deliberately chosen to plunge into "the abyss of the feminine sub-conscious," just as Faulkner in his greatest books is driven—where he does not flee to the mind of idiots—to look for his last word in the hearts of women. Where the antirational novel is not a Tale Told by an Idiot it is one told by a female. Miss Richardson, however, *lives* (as John Cowper Powys was the first to notice) in the "abyss" to which Joyce or Faulkner only strategically resort; and her example reminds us of the sense in which the whole "stream of consciousness" movement is a return from an exaggeratedly masculine literature to a feminine one. Wherever fiction turns from outdoors to indoors, from field to boudoir, from flight to love, from action to analysis, from reason to sensibility the female *persona* becomes, even for male authors, an inevitable mouthpiece; and the female author assumes—as in the novel's earliest decades—first importance. It is scarcely an accident that not only in its beginning were the chief figures of the twentieth-century experimental novel largely women; but that they continued overwhelmingly (Kay Boyle, Djuna Barnes, Katherine Anne Porter, Carson McCullers, and Eudora Welty come to mind) to be so, as that movement blurs out, becomes part of what the novel is generally presumed to be.

Miss Richardson expresses through one of her characters a certain disdain for "the way all down through the ages men have labelled their sexual impulses 'woman'. . ." and, indeed, her whole book is fraught with an embattled feminism. That such feminism and a resurgence of "feminine prose" go hand in hand (in Mrs. Woolf, for instance, as well as Miss Richardson) should surprise no one aware that the rise of the novel and a self-conscious movement aimed at changing the status of women arise together in the Western world. The desire to give the female her due and the resolve to grant new dignity to the impulsive life are hopelessly entangled, since Woman, for better or worse, stands—not only, as Miss Richardson seems to feel, for sexuality—but for the whole of man's undermind, the nonrational self which the eighteenth century called the Heart and which we call the id. Even Miss Richardson cannot pretend finally to treat men and women as mere facts of biology or sociology; in her fiction, too, they play "incompatible" symbolic roles, act out a mythic encounter.

"Men to make," she writes in *Dimple Hill,* "and women to love that which is made . . . If making things is humanity's highest spiritual achievement, then women *are* secondary . . . But *is* making pictures and bridges, and thumbscrews, humanity's highest achievement?" Miss Richardson is here, however, on the edge of a trap of her own contriving; for writing a book is, as ordinarily understood at least, precisely the sort of "making" which she describes as men's province. And that "loving" which she attributes to women must surely be done not in words but in silence —at the stable point of inner stillness; not art but contemplation be "humanity's highest achievement" and the aim of her lifework. It is, finally, I think, her awareness of this trap and her refusal to fall into it which give her book its peculiar quality, its inordinate length and the very "dulness" which we began by trying to define; for she *is* attempting, we realize at last, to write something which transcends the novel: an extended equivalent of the moment of silent communion between the human spirit and the world; and it takes many more words to indicate a silence than to make a noise.

What has been needed all along is a sensitive, patient and tactful explication of the whole of Miss Richardson's *Pilgrimage,* so that the random connoisseur can know where in the over-all pattern his sample comes, how it has all begun and even how, without surprises or reversals, it ends! This kind of explication Mr. Blake's study provides, pointing the reader toward the real and otherwise unavailable pleasures of Dorothy Richardson.

Contents

CHAPTER I

A Tour Amongst the Properties

I

FORD MADOX FORD once complained that Dorothy M. Richardson is the most abominably unknown modern writer and attributed the obscurity of her vast lifework *Pilgrimage* to critics' and readers' distaste for distinguished writing. The reasons for her neglect may be more various than Ford's complaint allows, but it is true that the novel is little read. Most histories of modern fiction acknowledge the importance of *Pilgrimage* as an early experiment in stream-of-consciousness fiction, or, more sympathetically, as a remarkable achievement in itself. But it is not generally read.

Perhaps there is something forbidding about a novel which, at its completion, consisted of twelve volumes, the first published in 1915 and the last in 1938.[1] If it be added that this long novel is concerned throughout with a single major character, a young Englishwoman, and is written entirely in the now familiar mode of stream-of-consciousness, it is possible that the demands on a reader of such a work may account partly for its neglect.

It is possible that the obscurity of *Pilgrimage* resulted

from the confusion of early reviewers and critics, who, misled by the prolonged publication of its parts and its "new" method, were ignorant of the book's intent. The fate of Ford's own *The Good Soldier* is parallel, though the books are scarcely similar as novels. Reviewers so misunderstood Ford's book, and hence damned its technique by misconstruing it, that the book was neglected as a failure for years. In Miss Richardson's case, the "new" way of writing (which stream-of-consciousness was in England in 1915) had to be learned by the same critics and readers. While they were adjusting their attitudes and values to the early Joyce and Richardson, more volumes of *Pilgrimage* appeared; the consequent critical uncertainty reflected in reviews is clear. The uncertainty of Miss Richardson's terminus for the novel as more and more volumes appeared —none an "end" in an ordinary sense—compounded the difficulty. Before the twelfth volume appeared in 1938 many readers had despaired, some had dismissed the work altogether impatiently, and others—Proust and most of Joyce and Woolf now assimilated—saw a lesser tributary, too long running, in the stream-of-consciousness experiment. Surely, reading parts of a novel intermittently during twenty-three years made a conception of the whole difficult; a consequent judgment of the whole was equally challenging.

There were some readers, of course, who recognized in the early volumes the import of Miss Richardson's technique and spoke of it as distinguished writing. May Sinclair, herself a novelist of considerable reputation at the time, defended Miss Richardson's books against the complaint that they had "no art and no method and no form." Miss

Sinclair attempted one of the earliest descriptions of Miss Richardson's method in terms of the demands of "stream of consciousness."[2] More precisely than Miss Sinclair, Constance Rourke described the method of the first books as "more than a centralization of narrative within a single point of view. . . . Even more positively than in the novels with which James deals, the material seems transposed from life itself, with all the inevitable irregularity of shape, without the creative rearrangement which James demands."[3] With unusual perception Miss Rourke sensed the intent as well as the method, commenting on the subtle notation of the growing-up process in which the heroine is portrayed. Pursuing another line of interest, Babette Deutsch described Miss Richardson's style as the techniques of imagistic poetry used with distinction in the novel.[4]

There were to be other sympathetic critics as more of the novel appeared and its shape became more apparent, but the demurrers seemed more numerous. The critical response to the first parts of the novel expressed an apparently genuine interest in the "new" writing but, not always perceiving its intent, distrusted it. A reviewer describing himself as "an elderly male" complained: "But we are the children of our generation, and it is hard, even for those who have learnt in middle age to delight in Mr. Conrad, to acquiesce without reserve in the ultra-Modernism of the new formula invented by Miss Richardson."[5] For him, reading *The Tunnel* after reading a Victorian romance was like "listening to a Jazz-band after a symphony by Mozart."[6] For another early reviewer, there was no justification for the "meaningless" difficulty and obscurity of these books, and besides: "Miss Richardson is recognized as a writer whose method is original; but in so far as that method consists of writing telegraphese, and putting words by themselves with full stops after them, it is not to be commended."[7] There were even paradoxical opinions that the books succeeded with "something," but in spite of themselves: "Written in a rapid succession of jerks and gasps, with words and stops and fragments of sentences shaken, one might say, out of a pepper pot— the breathless ejaculations of one who has run a mile to deliver some exciting news—the book succeeds, through the author's intensity of feeling and thought, in conveying (in defiance of all the laws of good writing) a clear impression of the girl and of the society at Newlands."[8]

Distinguished to some, distasteful to others, *Pilgrimage* required consideration on its own terms, a consideration impossible to the many who were unprepared for its technique. The novel subjected readers to the multiple and fluid impressions, reactions, contemplations of Miriam Henderson, a young British woman who, in the first chapters,[9] is a teacher in a German girls' school, then a resident teacher at the Misses Perne's school, Wordsworth House, in London. Leaving there after a vaguely dissatisfying year, she becomes the governess in the home of the Corries, a wealthy, "social" family living at Newlands. There is no plot in the conventional sense, no contour of clearly defined beginnings and endings of episodes, for it is only the heroine's reactions to people, places, things, ideas, and impulses that concerned the author. The reader thus gets only a refracted view of Miriam's experiences. Whatever he knows about what happens in Miriam's experiences, he knows only through her consciousness of it. To give this consciousness its way, Miss Richardson violated some linguistic and rhetorical conventions as well as conventions of narration. These departures were radical enough to discomfit the elderly male reviewer and to bewilder the critic who perceived a "success" in spite of the novelist's defiance of "the laws of good writing."

The critical fortunes of *Pilgrimage* were not to remain unchanged. By 1915, when *Pointed Roofs* was published, Proust's *Du côté de chez Swann* (1913) and Joyce's *Portrait of the Artist as a Young Man* (1914) had also appeared. Together, these novelists represented a sharp break with the generally familiar tradition of the novel, and became known as the subjective realists. In 1922 J. Middleton Murry summarized the effect of this break by imagining these subjectivists to say:

They [the great novelists of the past] endure in so far as they have rendered their own consciousness of life. Not the stories they told but the comprehensive attitude to life embodied in their stories makes them important to us today. Then why not abolish the mechanism of the story completely, if the end to which it is a means can be achieved without it? And there is more than this. A story seems necessarily to involve a falsification, a distortion of the reality. Life does not shape itself into stories; much less does our individual and unique consciousness lend itself to complete expression by means of an invented plot. Let us do away with this illusory objectivity, this imposition of completeness and order upon the incomplete and chaotic. All that we can know is our own experience, and the closer we keep to the immediate quality of that experience, the nearer shall we be to truth.[10]

There is, of course, a great deal more to be said in defining the character, causes, and effects of this revolt, but for our purposes here perhaps it is enough to note that by the 1920's the "new" writing was sufficiently understood to seem less enigmatic and more challenging critically.

By 1925 Dorothy Richardson had published the eighth chapter of *Pilgrimage*. In these chapters, Miriam, despairing of a continued teaching career, leaves the Corries, attends her dying mother, returns to London, takes a job as secretary to a group of Wimpole Street dentists, becomes friend to a variety of strange but engaging men and women, explores socialism, and falls in love with a Russian Jew whom she will not marry. The novel, now better understood, invited more critically acute questions than the early reviewers could have formulated: Must there not be some end to the flowing on and on of Miriam's experiences, an end dictated by some over-all structural pattern for the novel, if it is to be considered seriously as art? If the novel is to have some significant meaning as a "reading of life," should not that meaning emerge in a structure where some selective value operates? When critics complained now about Miss Richardson's technique, they were no longer distressed by stream-of-consciousness narrative itself, but by her use of it. Lawrence Hyde focused the problem clearly in a full essay on *Pilgrimage*. Granting the value and skill of Miss Richardson's exploitation of the vagaries of consciousness, Hyde nevertheless objects that the reader, "though delighted by the art with which these inner experiences are reproduced, ultimately becomes oppressed by the infinitude of loose ends out of which the whole is woven."[11] Hyde modified his objections by hoping, since the novel was not yet complete, that there would appear in later chapters a more "complete justification for the writing of those which have appeared up to the present, raising them from the status of a psychological dossier (albeit a fascinatingly interesting one) to that of an introduction inevitable for the appreciation of the state of illumination [to] which the experiences described in them could so well lead."

When the last four chapters were appearing between 1927 and 1938, it seemed to some critics that the thing hoped for in Hyde's essay was at last emerging. Miriam, now approaching thirty (she was seventeen in *Pointed Roofs*), has matured into a critical socialist, is unwilling to accept a second suitor's proposal of marriage, begins writing literary reviews, becomes the mistress of a celebrated literary figure, verges on a nervous breakdown, and seeking rest and resolution during an extended holiday, in the last chapter is a postulant Quaker. Even before the final volume was published, John Cowper Powys wrote a monograph on *Pilgrimage* in which he viewed Miriam's life as a "sort of Quest of the Holy Graal . . . the divine object of the ecstatic contemplative life, nothing less than the Beatific Vision; and not merely for that alone, for she is looking for this as it manifests itself, in diffused glory, throughout the whole inflowing and outflowing tide of phenomena."[12] To achieve this fictionally, Powys suggests, Miss Richardson has made of Miriam a symbol of universal human experience. Miriam's experiences, and the technique of the novel, achieve "nothing more nor less than a very deep and original system of life based upon a mystical quietude, an intensity of entranced, receptive contemplation."

Powys' suggestions are highly provocative. Apparently

the novel so prolonged in its completion and hence uncertain in its shape was beginning to suggest a unifying
theme for its complex detail. Joseph Warren Beach devoted
a chapter to *Pilgrimage* in his study of twentieth-century
fiction, and while his chief concern was with the novel's
distinction as impressionist, imagist fiction, he too posited
tentatively an interpretation of its meaning. He observes
that philosophical implications and intimations recur in
all the books, and adds: "Miriam is, we gather, on a
pilgrimage to some elusive shrine, glimpsed here and there
and lost to view. She is after something variously indicated from point to point, as reality, beauty, happiness, 'the
shine on things,' the 'little coloured garden.' "[13] The religious and philosophical language of Powys' and Beach's
interpretations implies for *Pilgrimage* a meaning which, in
view of the scope of experiences involved there, suggests a
life quest, a spiritual journey in search of the reality of the
world and of the self. The novel, to them, was clearly more
than an elaborately extended grouping of Miriam's impressions. A shape, purposive and meaningful, was revealing
itself.

The suggestions of Powys and Beach have not been
developed fully in later writings about *Pilgrimage*.[14] During all the years of its accomplishment, the reader has
wanted, needed to know the significance of the experiences
to which the novel subjects him. There is necessarily an
assumption about the nature of the reality of life for Miss
Richardson, and with it an assumption about the life-art
relation, which would inform our reading of her novel.
Definition of the life value underlying the kind and extent
of experiences included in the book, as well as of the

method of screening those experiences through the consciousness of a particular young woman, is needed to make clear the character of this novel. For, contingent on the meaning which a reader perceives to unify this elaborate fiction, there is a structural pattern—however loose or "irregular" or minimal—designed to approximate and reveal that meaning. If this relationship between meaning and structure is defined, it may also appear that Miss Richardson's technique, frequently asserted to be an excellence apart, is integral to the patterning of the novel as a whole. Reading *Pilgrimage* analytically as a single book, we may be able to define its meaning as a criticism of life, describe the structure which supports that meaning, and relate the book's style to the design of the whole.

2

Miss Richardson herself did not say much about these matters. Apparently a reticent, withdrawn woman in respect to statements about herself or her work, she wrote little that may be taken as a declared aesthetic or theory of the novel. There are a few essays, reviews, and notes in literary journals, but nowhere a systematic creed. From what she did write, however, we may infer several ideas which should be suggestive in studying *Pilgrimage*.

Asked to define her conception of literary art for a biographical dictionary of modern authors, Miss Richardson replied: "Literature is a product of the stable human consciousness, enriched by experience and capable of deliberate, concentrated contemplation."[15] There is little precision in this statement; indeed it scarcely defines the nature or function of literary art at all. It does hint at the source of literary creation, but it does not specify the process. The hint in the phrase "stable human consciousness" gives pause, although its meaning is vague until one reads:

Definitions of consciousness vary from school to school and are necessarily as incomplete as definitions of life. The only satisfactory definition of a man's consciousness is his life. And this, superficially regarded, does exhibit a sort of stream-line. But the consciousness sits stiller than a tree. "The mind" may be or become, anything from a rag-bag to a mad-house. It may wobble continuously or may be more or less steadily focused. But its central core, luminous point (call it what you will, its names are legion), tho more or less continuously expanding to maturity, remains stable, one with itself thruout life.

We are still not sure of the meaning of consciousness. It is equivalent to the life of an individual. But it is also his "central core" or "luminous point," and yet distinct from mind. There seems to be some indefiniteness in her use of the word "life." If we interpolate a distinction between "life" as the vital center, "luminous point" of a man's psychic being, and "existence" as his outward, behavioral being in the world, Miss Richardson seems to say, simply, that the life of any individual is a stable, receptive center of awareness which may be called his consciousness. She says further:

We all date our existence from our first conscious awareness of reality outside ourselves. And this awareness is direct and immediate, *preceding* instruction as to the nature of the realities by which we are surrounded. Instruction and experience can enrich and deepen but can never outdo or replace this first immediate awareness. It recurs in different forms, thruout life.

Consciousness is a center of awareness, instinctive to man, immediately and directly—perhaps mystically—perceiving the reality outside himself, and never losing its primal vision. What accrues to the individual through instruction and experience in the world intrudes, as it were, between the individual and a reality which transcends phenomena. The fact that the initial awareness of reality "recurs in different forms, thruout life" suggests that the sense of reality is awakened or heightened in the individual if he will but seek it in the midst of the great flux of learned or experienced phenomena which constitute existence. The technique is deliberate, concentrated contemplation of the center of the self. And because the experience is possible for every man, it is this potential which, Dorothy Richardson says, provides the basis of the literary experience for writer and reader.

Is not this consciousness the sole link between reader and writer? The writer's (and the reader's) brain may be "on fire," his imagination may construct this and that, but the contemplative center remains motionless. Does not the power and the charm of all literature, from the machine-made product to the "work of art," from the book which amuses or instructs to the one which remakes the world and ourselves (*why* do we recognize it?) reside in its ability to rouse and to concentrate the reader's contemplative consciousness?

May we not infer that the writer is somehow specially endowed with a clarity of perception and a technical facility in representing it which distinguish him from other men? If so, the reader is able, through literature, to recall his own awareness of reality, and to acknowledge—or deny— the writer's vision according as it is "true" and satisfying.

The crucial choice for the reader depends on the attitude *toward* reality which an author inevitably reveals. This is the author himself revealed, according to Miss Richardson, and thus every work of literature is a signed self-portrait of the artist, revealing, whether directly or by implication, and whatever his method of approach, the artist's tastes, prejudices, and philosophy.

Miss Richardson's ideas about literature, as presented here, bear more heavily on speculations in psychology and philosophy than on specific problems of literary technique. These ideas have established, however, a basis for exploring her view of life and its meaning as the essential communication between writer and reader. But for us the important life-art relation which *Pilgrimage* implements requires a similar basis for exploring the modes of illusion with which *Pilgrimage* achieves aesthetic coherence and purpose. A fundamental question persists: What *is* reality in Dorothy Richardson's view? And, ultimately: What does this reality require of the novelist who would achieve its illusion?

Again, Miss Richardson gave us only hints toward an answer in writings other than *Pilgrimage*. For the 1938 collected edition of the novel, she wrote a brief, subtle foreword which is her only public account of the book, and which guides the reader to certain of her beliefs about *Pilgrimage* and fiction generally.

She acknowledges a tradition of modern realistic fiction and identifies Balzac as its father. Balzac's subjective identification with his material—however "objective" and "typical" his conceptions—through sympathies and attitudes qualifies him, in Miss Richardson's mind, as a realist. She takes no specific account of Flaubert, the Goncourts, Maupassant, or Zola, but alludes to Balzac's successors whose English line is typified by Arnold Bennett. Balzac and Bennett, "while representing . . . the turning of the human spirit upon itself, may be called realists by nature and unawares."[16] The meaning of this judgment is not clear until Miss Richardson adds: "They believe themselves to be substituting, for the telescopes of the writers of romance whose lenses they condemn as both rose-coloured and distorting, mirrors of plain glass."[17]

The image is striking. The realists distinguished subject and object in such a way as to impute to objects a reality significant in itself. Through plain glass one sees only phenomenal, objective existence; and this is no mirror at all. The outward-looking devices of their method are their failure. Reality, properly mirrored, would be an image of the self, an inward-looking view of the beholder. Virginia Woolf's famous essay "Mr. Bennett and Mrs. Brown" clarifies the practical significance of the same complaint by challenging the realism of Wells, Galsworthy, and Bennett. Mrs. Woolf complained that realistic fiction had no characters—only things, institutions, gestures. "For what, after all," she says, "is character—the way that Mrs. Brown, for instance, reacts to her surroundings—when we cease to believe what we are told about her, and begin to search out her real meaning for ourselves?"[18] With equal conviction Miss Richardson believes that the realists' deceptive mirrors have misled them into concentration on "man versus conditions impeached as the authors of his discontent," and thus into preoccupation with "satire and protest, and every form of conventionalized human association."[19] To her, this was not realism.

Thus, in 1911 she began *Pilgrimage* as an experiment:

a "feminine equivalent" to the "current masculine realism" just described.[20] Feminine reality was to be the contemplated subjective life which her definition of literature describes. Reality—"real reality," Virginia Woolf called it—was ideal reality; subject and object in experience ultimately were significant only in terms of the subject's consciousness of object. What, then, should be represented in the realistic novel but an individual's consciousness of the world of phenomena? The inner life is the reality, and that must be the material of fiction which creates the illusion of reality. The problem of an adequate form for representing this reality was ancillary.

The orthodox novel was unsatisfactory to Miss Richardson. In a review of Joyce's *Finnegans Wake* she describes the development of the modern novel and reminds us that, historically, the novel was a story-telling function with scarcely more than a story demanded by the reader.

. . . stories whose power to enthrall resided chiefly in their ability to provide both excitement and suspense; uncertainty as to what, in the pages still to be turned, might befall the hero from whom all too soon, returning to the "world of everyday," the reader must regretfully take leave.[21]

In another essay on fiction, she remarked that the new novel (meaning the stream-of-consciousness novel), when it began, wanted to avoid

. . . the vast discrepancy between the actuality of life as experienced and the dramatic fatalism, shared in spite of its relative freedom from the time-limit, by the orthodox novel with the stage; the way, akin to that of science, it must not only lift its selected material from the context of reality but

what is even more decisively restrictive, must ignore, in order
to supply a story complete with beginning, middle, climax,
and curtain, the always unique modifications of contingency.[22]

Unrestricted by formal conventions of plot, the novel of
feminine realism should be equally free of open or in-
ferential essayistic purpose. Miss Richardson objects to
conventional forms and conventional means of purposive
selection on the grounds that neither has any real counterpart in life as experienced. Thus she rejects what had been
the staples of aesthetic form for the novelist, and implies
that the realistic novel must be fundamentally mimetic, its
value as art consisting primarily, though not exclusively, in
the resemblance between "felt life" and its illusion in the
author's mode of narration.

One effect of these differences between orthodox and
"new" novels would be the similarity of the subjective
novel and poetry:

Opening, just anywhere, its pages, the reader is immediately
engrossed. Time and place, and the identity of characters, if
any happen to appear, are relatively immaterial. Something
may be missed. Incidents may fail of their full effect through
ignorance of what has gone before. . . . He finds himself
within a medium whose close texture, like that of poetry, is
everywhere significant and although, when the tapestry hangs
complete before his eyes, each portion is seen to enhance the
rest and the shape and the intention of the whole grows clear,
any single strip may be divorced from its fellows without
losing everything of its power and of its meaning.[23]

The image of the tapestry hanging complete clearly suggests that Miss Richardson did not wish to dispense altogether with coherence and meaning and purpose. But she

did conceive of their content differently. According to her, the rendering of consciousness in a work of fiction is the portrayal of life. We may infer that, this being true, the coherence and meaning of the data of consciousness as they are integrated within attitudes or beliefs about the world and the self imply the meaning and coherence of the novel. The process of such integration is a process in time; hence, the psychic development of an individual toward discovery or fulfillment may be the purposive control of the novel. The reality communicated is the reality of felt experience, itself meaningful only in terms of the deeper self discovered.

Thus *Pilgrimage* was begun experimentally in 1911 and consistently developed until its completion in 1938. Miss Richardson's demand in 1911 for a "new" novel adequate to her own "new" vision seems to reflect the general restless iconoclasm that characterizes much of British intellectual life at the beginning of this century. The general ferment of thought in religion, politics, economics, ethics, and art between 1890 and 1910 was the environment in which Dorothy Richardson came to her literary career. The foundations of civilized life, so certain and stable for most of the Victorians, were shaken, redefined, realigned under the promises of the "new" philosophies, the "new" psychology, the "new" social and political theory. Idealists and liberals, socialists and feminists, prophets and reformers at once created and reflected the atmosphere of revolt, change, experiment. And frequently the foremost among these spokesmen were writers who, like Shaw and Wells, were at the center of particular movements in the new order. A sensitive young author—especially a young woman, since the role of woman herself was as stringently revaluated as anything—had to locate himself in this environment. Dorothy Richardson's middle-class origin, her disenchantment with its value, her subsequent efforts at intellectual and social reorientation as an emancipated woman, her early, close association with Wells and his coterie seem to define in part her identity with and participation in that environment. The distillation of her experiences during her formative years emerges as the new vision to be represented in a new novel—both to be comprehended under what she called "feminine realism."

But she was not alone in her special preoccupations. The direction of her vision was, apparently, that which Proust, Joyce, and later, Mrs. Woolf also found. The influence of Bergson's philosophy, James's studies in thought-experience, and later, Freud's clinical explorations of inner life drew these writers to a common pursuit in fiction. And, ultimately, they shared the legacy of the nineteenth-century romantic poets and the French Symbolists, conjoining several intellectual and aesthetic developments that produced Yeats and Eliot as well as Proust, Richardson, and Joyce.[24] But these subjective novelists began their work independently of each other. Miss Richardson records that she thought she was embarking on a "lonely path," only to find later that she was in the midst of a populous highway.

She did know the work of Henry James, however. It may therefore seem curious that she should speak of a new novel breaking so radically with orthodox fiction around 1911, when James's achievement in English fiction preludes, as it were, the psychological novel. James had antici-

pated some of the subjectivists' motivations as early as his
1884 essay, "The Art of Fiction." In that essay James remarked: "A Novel is in its broadest definition a personal, a
direct impression of life: that, to begin with, constitutes its
value, which is greater or less according to the intensity of
the impressions." His strictures on the assumption that
adventure has to be action, surprise, and the like; his argument that experience is never limited or complete, but is
rather an "immense sensibility"; his insistence that "form"
should be appreciated after the fact of the impressions for
which it is a vehicle—all seem to prefigure Miss Richardson's own view of the novel. In the Foreword to *Pilgrimage*
she does acknowledge a "far from inconsiderable technical
influence" from James. But Miriam (who surely speaks for
Dorothy Richardson) in *Dawn's Left Hand* tells Hypo, the
"advanced" critic: "Even as you . . . revel in all the ways
James uses to reveal the process of civilizing Chad, you are
distracted from your utter joy by fury over all he is unaware of. And even Conrad. The self-satisfied, complacent,
know-all condescendingness of their handling of their
material. . . . The torment of *all* novels is what is left
out."[25]

The technical strategy of James's "point of view" no
doubt appealed to Miss Richardson; she expressly compli-
ments his prose style "demanding . . . a perfection of sustained concentration."[26] But his "vast tracts of urbane
commentary" were, after all, an "enclosed resounding
chamber where no plant grows and no mystery pours in
from the unheeded stars." James, to her, shared with the
orthodox novelists the error of exclusion: the consciousness
of James's single observer was truncated; too much of what

constitutes a sensitive awareness of the vast, mysterious world was lost in James's exquisite moral preoccupations. Because of this limitation, James was "a venerable gentleman, a charmed and charming high priest of nearly all the orthodoxies, inhabiting a softly lit enclosure he mistook, until 1914, for the universe."[27]

For her, then, there was still the challenge of a novel where independently assertive reality could appear adequately within a text.

3

One thing which Miss Richardson did like about James's point-of-view strategy was that it introduces the reader of the novel to the "drama" therein without taking him, before it begins, "upon a tour amongst the properties." This preliminary discussion of *Pilgrimage* has been such a tour. The novel's critical fortunes, its author's conception of literature and the literary experience, her motivations to write it, the milieu of her ambitions—these are, after all, properties functional only for the production itself. They suggest lines of interest, however, for a reading of *Pilgrimage* which will describe specifically its character as a novel.

Such a reading will necessitate an analysis of the entire accumulation of the heroine Miriam Henderson's experiences as narrated so that we can determine, first, what the significance of those experiences is through her reactions to them; and second, what view of life or reality Miss Richardson communicates through her presentation of Miriam's reactions. We will assume that experience has primarily a subjective reality, and that in the stream-of-consciousness novel the author inevitably reveals a thematic view of experience. The time spread of the novel (more than a decade) achieves a dynamic, developing experience-consciousness relationship, rather than a static, reflexive one. Hence, the analysis will trace the stages of development of Miss Richardson's life view as those stages are implied in the development of Miriam's consciousness. The effect of her experiences is to achieve self-discovery, or the reality of identity in Miss Richardson's terms. The meaning of *Pilgrimage* will be apparent, therefore, in its "reading of life" through Miriam's impressions of, and reactions to, life. The analysis of meaning will imply a definite structural pattern in the novel and will give us a basis for analyzing the technique[28] Miss Richardson employed.

We may then be able to conclude that *Pilgrimage*, recently discussed again as an enigma of form and meaning,[29] has both coherence and integrity as a novel.

CHAPTER II

The Shape of Shapelessness

THE STREAM-OF-CONSCIOUSNESS novel, whatever else its distinctive merits may be, succeeded in giving the reader greater access to the persons in the fiction. It is true that Henry James had evolved a method of narration which allowed a "sharper specification of the signs of life," but the psychological novelists, believing themselves possessed, beyond James, of a fuller grasp of what life itself is, seized upon the individual consciousness as the sharpest specification of personal identity.[1] Attention to the consciousness not only identified the person; it comprehended the "world" where the world mattered.

The results were various, for the psychological novelist determined, according to his thematic and technical problems, whether the identity of a character ought to be regarded as a realized personality, gradually revealed, or a personality shown in the process of its own development. The choice of exploiting or developing a consciousness, the one inevitably involving the other but one or the other dominating, depended on the purposes of the entire novel structure. Virginia Woolf portrays Clarissa Dalloway as a woman who *is* something on a particular day, and while it is true that Mrs. Dalloway of that day is the sum of her past, retrospectively compassed, she is essentially "undeveloping" in the time duration of *Mrs. Dalloway,* only changing significantly at the very last of the novel in its thematic fulfillment. It is Stephen Dedalus' development which concerned James Joyce. The interior time duration of *Portrait of the Artist as a Young Man* permits the definition, in successive periods of time, of the stages involved in the *becoming* of Stephen, artist.

For Dorothy Richardson it is important equally to exploit what Miriam Henderson is at specific times, and to show what, at the same times, she is becoming, for Miss Richardson's theory of personality admits two fundamentals: first, that there is a self or quality of being which is not phenomenal in origin, but is a manifestation at a point in time and space of a timeless, universal self; and second, that there is a personality or self-consciousness which develops for an individual through the accretion and interpenetration of experience.

The second of these ideas is a commonplace of modern psychology, but the first is outside psychology's province: it is a theory of the speculative philosopher. Regarding personality as the unified self, the psychologist is concerned about an integrating or unifying development that harmonizes feeling and perception, inner concerns and outer realities in the individual, but he works within the possibilities of the manifest personality.[2] The speculative philosopher, positing a self beyond the phenomenal one, can identify it as the Infinite or Absolute in the finite person, or, in religious terms, the divine immanent in man. The unity or harmony of personality, then, may be the adjustment of the manifest self to the transcendent self. Feeling—the intuitive, valuating center of awareness—originates in the urgings of the divine spirit in an individual; perception— his sensible access to the phenomenal world—is the means of a developing consciousness. It is possible to express this idea in terms of subliminal or subconscious life and conscious life as well. In this view the integration of personality, the sense of one's reality or identity, is the harmonizing of perception and feeling, the adjustment of dynamic, human becoming to stable, divine being.

The outlines of this view of personality or self-realization are clearly the rudiments of transcendental, mystical belief. Specifically, it is the theoretical framework on which one of the foremost modern interpreters of Quaker mysticism has developed a conception of the meaning of personality. For Rufus M. Jones, and the Friends, personality is an achievement, a thing realizing itself, implementing the will to be. The goal of the process, admitting its fundamentally important route through instructive social interrelations, is spiritual consciousness, which the Quakers believe to be the mystical experience of God in the individual and, through contemplation, its manifestation in "motor-effects" (Jones's usage) for the person in his society. The *felt* presence of God is the achievement of unified personality, for that presence is the reality which harmonizes its urgings (as feeling) and the cognitions of perception.[3]

This is by no means a comprehensive summary of modern Quaker thought, but it is sufficient to indicate the outline of a theory of personality which Dorothy Richardson apparently adopted. Miss Richardson's own study of Quakerism[4] does not define theoretical positions explicitly;

it is a kind of appreciation essay. But her acknowledgment of the influence of the Jones study cited here allows us to assume that the Quaker view of personality will help us to understand Miriam Henderson as an intelligible character in a work of fiction, and to understand the "reading of life" which her elaborate characterization is designed to give.

The twelve volumes of *Pilgrimage* compass the manifold experiences that show the *becoming* of Miriam and its reconciliation to the *being* that she must acknowledge in order to achieve a sense of the reality of identity and its consequent vision of the reality of life. The massive detail —some trivial and tiresome though functional; some profoundly suggestive of broad analysis and interpretation— is only secondarily important in itself: perhaps important in the sense of Dorothy Richardson's Miriam Henderson's "eye-view of the world," a *"Comédie Humaine* of English speaking Europe."[5] It is indeed possible to read *Pilgrimage* with great profit as a vast critical commentary on humanity, society, art, religion, the English character. But the primary importance of the detail is its cumulative effect on the perceiving mind, as that mind seeks a perspective adequate to its demand for reality. Miriam is seventeen in *Pointed Roofs,* where she begins her life quest. In *Dimple Hill* she is over thirty. The years between, as selected for the novel, are crowded with great and minor experiences; some occur and pass quickly, flashing only momentarily a telling insight but residually important in future experiences; others occur and recur, modified by time and memory, and remain in the foreground of Miriam's consciousness as impetus to thought and action. Upon Miss Richardson's own advice, the reader can open the novel anywhere and find engrossment in the "close texture," poetically rendered, of these experiences.

Beneath this quantity of complex detail, however, there are qualitative currents which define the developing consciousness successively in movements from youth and innocence to maturity and wisdom; from disillusioning conformity to enlightened individuality; from the opposition of feeling and thought to their reconciliation in belief; from dismay at life and the world to joy and wonder at life and the world transformed by the realized self. Miriam's stream of experience flows into larger currents persisting beneath the surface—at first separate, then conflicting, occasionally converging—themselves channelized finally in an achieved mystical vision.

I

In the first three chapters of *Pilgrimage—Pointed Roofs, Backwater, Honeycomb*—the reader meets Miriam Henderson, learns something of her essential character, and witnesses developments in her young adult life which motivate her extended pilgrimage and which provide the later conflictive movements of the novel. In *Pointed Roofs* the initial, circumstantial cause of Miriam's first independent journey into life is her father's financial collapse, a crisis serious enough to require radical readjustment of the Henderson family's life. Miriam, third of four daughters, with an impressive resoluteness vaguely disturbing to her sisters, determines to "make her own way" and accepts a job as teacher in a girls' school at Hanover, Germany. A middle-class background, an education normal for an English girl of that class in the 1890's, a nagging distress

at her intellectual deficiency, her plainness, her "unsoci-
ableness," and a lack of "religion" (so her sister Eve complained) are what we know about Miriam as she leaves
for Hanover. Self-assurance and independent assertiveness distinguish Miriam among her sisters, but when alone
she is full of self-effacing doubts, sensitivities, and fears.

At Fräulein Pfaff's school, Miriam allays many of her
misgivings in her happy absorption in the new life. She
fascinates the reader with her extraordinary receptivity to
fine impressions of people, places, objects, sounds. She
seems especially happy in the presence of natural scenery,
the quaint charm of the German town ("pointed roofs");
she is genuinely ecstatic when listening to music. So ecstatic, in fact, that the reader is somewhat nonplused to
share this kind of reaction at the first *Vorspielen* among
the girls:

Emma Bergmann was playing. The single notes of the
opening *motif* of Chopin's Fifteenth Nocturne fell pensively
into the waiting room. Miriam, her fatigue forgotten, slid to
a featureless freedom. It seemed to her that the light with
which the room was filled grew brighter and clearer. She felt
that she was looking at nothing and yet was aware of the
whole room like a picture in a dream. Fear left her. The
human forms all round her lost their power. They grew
suffused and dim. . . . The pensive swing of the music
changed to urgency and emphasis. . . . It came nearer and
nearer. It did not come from the candle-lit corner where the
piano was. . . . It came from everywhere. It carried her out
of the house, out of the world.
It hastened with her, on and on towards great brightness.
. . . Everything was growing brighter and brighter. (I, 42-43)

Miriam does not understand these transports; she worries and wonders if anyone around her shares this same sense. "It was everywhere, in the food, in the fragrance rising from the opened lid of the tea-urn . . .[6] It hung about the fabrics and fittings of the house. Overwhelmingly it came in through oblongs of window giving on to stairways. Going upstairs in the light pouring in from some un-curtained window she would cease for a moment to breathe." (I, 158)

To dismiss this kind of experience as psychophysical disruption or vestigial autism and to pass on is tempting, but it is unfair: we know too little about Miriam to con-clude that she is unbalanced. It is apparent only that she is essentially and consistently adolescent in several extrav-agances of feeling. The moments of exceptionally height-ened consciousness may or may not be more than that; they at least alert the reader to Miriam's unusual capacity for moments of involuntary psychic well-being.

The mystery of these feeling states is vexing to Miriam, and so is her vague discontent with "chapel" church as she has known it. She is clearly aware of some objections she has to religious orthodoxy, but she cannot define—or answer—her own objections; she merely protests. Sitting in the Schloss Kirche with the school girls, Miriam recoils from the sermon, its "unsound premises" calling for dis-agreement which she is not able or, worse, not privileged to give. When the congregation sings a familiar hymn, she reflects: " 'Nun-dank-et-al-le-Gott.' Now-thank-all-God. She read that first line again and felt how much better the thing was without the 'we' and 'our.' " (I, 75) And as the Germans sang it, "it did not sound like a 'proc-

lamation' or an order. It was . . . somehow . . . everyday."
(I, 76) Because she is troubled about the nature of God,
albeit sophomorically, Miriam tends to throw all matters
of doctrine and worship under suspicion. The extent of
her concern is chiefly a fierce rebelliousness against
churches, preachers, complacently pious people. "Something" is wrong about people's notions of God and religion, something intrusive; even Christ seems somehow
intrusive.

The rebelliousness shows itself in Miriam's reaction to
conforming social behavior as well. Even in the matter of
directed walks for the entire school, she resents the rigidity
of a group, enjoying her "ever-recurring joyous sense of
emergence and her longing to go leisurely and alone . . . to
go on and on at first and presently to look." (I, 90) The
rebellion shades ominously into an attitude toward men:
"Something in their bearing and manner. . . . Blind and
impudent." (I, 167)

A tiresome girl and an unpromising heroine, we may
conclude. But for most of *Pointed Roofs,* Miriam is a
happy young girl, enjoying her friends and the life about
her; the dark broodings blend subtly into the texture of a
young girl's year in Germany. The reader is interested,
finally, in what can develop from both this lively joyousness and these spasmodic broodings.

The year at Hanover passes and, in *Backwater,* the next
year Miriam is at home again waiting to assume a new
position as resident teacher at Wordsworth House, the
Misses Perne's school in north London. At home, her essential *jeunesse* is very clear in the slangy sessions with
her sisters, their excited preparations for a party and for

the presence of favorite beaux, the exquisite excitement
of Miriam's first cigarette. But at Wordsworth House she
is again the troubled Miriam, discontent with her poverty
and plainness, apprehensive about most women and all
men, struggling with problems of faith and belief, but
still sustained by her moments of heightened feeling well-
ing up with or without external cause. The image of spring
now occurs to her whenever an "illumination" is upon her,
and in her consciousness it is equivalent to "the solitary
spring air." Miriam contemplates this inner experience and
is surprised that it is something that has occurred for as
long as she can remember, the first time as a child of six
walking along a garden path. The continuity of the experiences suggests to her that it is her "nearest most intimate self." (I, 282) She realizes, too, that she can sum-
mon the memory of a past illumination and withdraw, at
will, into the joy of the recalled experience.

This realization came partly out of necessity, for the
Banbury Park year is as bleak as the Hanover year was
happy. The drudgery of teaching—only sometimes relieved
by the awareness of sharing life with students—the drab,
cramped greyness of north London, her poverty and com-
monplaceness, the prospect of a lifetime of Banbury Park
—all oppress Miriam during the entire long term she serves
there. She seeks refuge in books, discovering Rosa Nouchette Carey and projecting herself into the domestic happiness described in Carey's novels. But she is frightened
and sometimes repelled by the kind of woman she would
become in that life. Then in Mrs. Hungerford she finds
the rich, gay social existence appealing, but despair returns
because she has no access to that world, nor any talent for

its rituals. She resolves to leave Banbury Park, for there could be only doom in its life.

Whatever is known to the reader of a stream-of-consciousness novel is known almost entirely as a character perceives it or thinks it, but the reader has the advantage of a double view: that of the perceiving consciousness in the novel, and his own view of those perceptions. The reader sometimes realizes much more about the thing perceived than the character himself, and of course much more about the character than he himself is aware of. This double view can be crucial in a novel like *Pilgrimage* where, by obvious design in the first chapters, the reader must evaluate Miriam's experiences and their effect on her in a way that she cannot, at this point in her life, evaluate them herself.

In *Backwater,* the reader begins to formulate a conflict which fundamentally organizes the panoramic impressions of Miriam's Hanover and Banbury Park years. It is clear that Miriam's illuminations—whether in the presence of streaming light, under the influence of music, among natural scenes, or through Wordsworthian recollections of past moments—in which she has a sense of good or beauty, are merely felt as a kind of psychic well-being, undifferentiated and imprecisely described. The sign is bright light and the stimuli are various, but their effect is always an ideal condition of the self. It is a condition not always—not even often—possible of attainment in the individual's social existence. The "solitary spring air" is divorced from the realities of north London; this fundamental disparity between feeling and perception is the conflict formulated but unresolved in *Backwater.*

But how, when one must live and function in a world of affairs, can one achieve the "solitary spring air" without taking refuge in silent isolation? Miriam's answer was not to be found at Wordsworth House, so with characteristic determination she seeks another mode of life which may provide the answer.

In *Honeycomb,* Miriam believes for a while that she has found it. She is now governess for the children of the Corries, a wealthy, "social" family living at Newlands. All past miseries of poverty and discomfort leave her, and with them the attendant worries about "deeper things." In the midst of wealth, easeful living, luxuriant surroundings, there is gratification in plenty for her sense of beauty and comfort. But the people at Newlands soon disillusion Miriam: Mrs. Corrie, chattering and flashing about, empty-headed, all gesture; the assorted inevitable house guests, complacent, forcing wit, snobbish, speaking as if to defend themselves against an accusation never made; the men, "hard angry bones," always thinking something, but only one thing at a time. Newlands was worldly life and Miriam was to prepare the Corrie children for it.

She envied and pitied and despised those lives. Envied the ease and despised the ignorance, the awful cruel struggle of society that they were growing up for—no joy, a career and sport for the boy, clubs, the weary dyspeptic life of the blasé man, and for the girl lonely cold hard bitter everlasting "social" life. She envied the ease. (I, 382)

The trouble with this kind of life was that nobody "was ever quite there, realizing." (I, 388)

At first Miriam regards her failure at Newlands as her

personal deficiency. Some lines of verse, learned long ago, keep coming to mind:

> Take each fair mask for what it shows itself
> Nor strive to look beneath it.

But this proves to be false counsel: "Taking each fair mask was a fine grown-up game." And when "spring" was upon her in those moments of clear good feeling, it was evident to her that "life is not a mask, it *is* fair; the gold in one's hair is real." (I, 392)

The "fair masks" of Newlands life must be, therefore, the signs of the falseness of that life, gauged by the sense of good within. The reality she sought, the something inside "deeper down . . . cool and fresh—endless garden" was not Newlands. (I, 425) Having attempted to merge feeling with this way of life, she had only misplaced it. She leaves, joins her family in preparations for the double wedding of her sisters Sarah and Harriett, activities which again and again bring the image of the "little coloured garden" and its sense of beauty, peace, contentment. She contemplates this peace:

> "Peace I give unto you, My peace I give unto you. Not as the world giveth, give I unto you—"
> Christ said that. But peace came from God—the peace of God that passeth all understanding. How could Christ give that? He put Himself between God and man. Why could not people get at God direct? He was somewhere.
>
> . . . .
>
> The Kingdom of Heaven is *within* you. But even Christ went about sad, trying to get people to do some sort of trick that He said was necessary before they could find God—some-

thing to do with Himself. There was something wrong about that.

If one were perfectly still, the sense of God was there. (I, 457-58)

The proximity of "the little coloured garden" and the "sense of God" is a tentative improvement for Miriam, momentarily offering relief from obsessive thoughts about her failure in the world, or the failure of the world itself by so much as it departs from her vague sense of "good."

Honeycomb ends with an episode which fairly summarizes the meaning of Miriam's first groping advance in her pilgrimage. The wedding over, she is left to confront the alarmingly advanced illness of her mother. Miriam takes her mother to a quiet resort and witnesses the daily deterioration of the ailing woman. One evening, in a moment of complete exhaustion from her long vigils, Miriam falls asleep, leaving her mother unattended. When she awakens, she is stunned to find that her mother, in defeat and despair, has committed suicide. The oppressive ugliness and bitterness of life is poignantly focused in this tragedy; the overwhelming realities of existence are symbolized in this death: "I am in eternity . . . where their worm dieth not and their fire is not quenched." (I, 490)

It was after reading these first chapters that some critics expressed regret that Miss Richardson had used her considerable talent on so unpromising a heroine. It is true that Miriam is adolescent in many of her attitudes and in much of her behavior: there is something distressingly familiar in her frequent flights to emotional finality and verbal superlatives in critical situations (she admired Mr. Corrie greatly until at dinner one evening he upset a pet belief of hers; she immediately hated him completely—and all men). And it is true that Miriam is sometimes rather too ecstatic about soap, soft lights, or hot tea. Her redeeming quality is the unusual sensitivity which she frequently shows for the beauty of nature and music, for the nuances of human gesture and expression. The potential of this capacity prevents the reader from condemning her as entirely dull. He remembers that Miriam is seventeen, eighteen, nineteen and that Miss Richardson is concerned to document the girl's growth of personality.

The evidences of growth are already apparent. Miriam at Newlands is clearly more discerning and articulate than Miriam in Hanover; what, for instance, was a pouting distrust of men in *Pointed Roofs* has begun to emerge in *Honeycomb* as distaste for the characteristic habit of masculine minds—"propositional" dogmatism. Similarly, for her "illuminations," her distress about religion, her self-deprecation, or her impatience with social sham or pretence, Miriam at the end of *Honeycomb* has begun to focus her own experiences through the perspective of as yet embryonic attitudes about individuality and the integrity of the self, social duty, relations between the sexes, the relationship of God and man—in a word, about the reality of life. With these developing attitudes, she resumes her quest for the "little coloured garden" in the world of affairs; *The Tunnel* and *Interim* are the next course in its fulfillment.

2

The tone of *The Tunnel* and *Interim* is set when Miriam declares early in the former that "I am back now where

I was before I began trying to do things like other people. I left home to get here." (II, 13) She is in London, living at Mrs. Bailey's rooming house and working as an assistant to some Wimpole Street dentists. If she regards her immediately past experiences as her failure in an "ordinary" life restricted by custom and convention, she can be happy in the thought that now she is free to be herself, free to confront the world on her own terms.

The advantages of this freedom are unmistakable. Miriam is in motion, physically among a variety of satisfying friendships and in excursions into London life; intellectually in the almost voracious eagerness with which she is learning things. At the Wilsons' (Alma Wilson is an old school friend, her husband a rising young literary figure) an altogether new perspective opens for her: the bright, literary, intellectual group who fascinate and challenge because they *think,* and dare to be different (she is thrilled that they are unsurprised—pleased, rather—at her smoking cigarettes). She listens to their talk, tries to remember their "brilliances," senses her own misgivings and disagreements, but cannot verbalize them. They talk of "life" and history and art and science; in their minds there is a sense of the relevance of things. Their attitudes are sometimes disturbing though; especially Hypo Wilson's, for he is the central figure in the group and the most engaging, but he seems always to think as a materialist, and so dogmatically. The agony of sensing that there is an answer for him, if she could only know it, intensifies Miriam's sense of inadequacy but also stimulates her urge to find the terms of her disagreement.

She reads diligently; although we do not always know

exactly what, the results are apparent in her conversations, allusions, and reveries. Rosa Nouchette Carey, Mrs. Hungerford, and Ouida have given way to a range of authors embracing both Shakespeare and Zola. She has undertaken philosophy, with the effect of an enlarged facility for pondering her chronic problems. She is able now to explore metaphysical problems with elementary understanding and firm conviction, even though there is faltering competence. For instance, she is capable of arguing for a very real distinction between what, logically, one cannot admit to possibility, and what, intuitively, one can. But the difference so astounds her that she rests in the emotional satisfaction of the experience, pursuing no consequent thought. (II, 93)

Often the center of such speculation is her concern about religion and churches. She persists in a sceptical concern about the nature of God—she seems never to doubt the fact of God—a concern inseparable from her distrust of the churches and their theologies. She rejects a theistic God as "a man's idea . . . Sitting on a throne judging everybody and passing sentence, is a thing a man would do." (II, 94) Besides, the idea of eternal punishment makes God "a fool and a failure." If humanity is wicked, then God is: "You can't separate God and humanity, and that includes women who don't really believe any of those things." (II, 94) A pantheistic God appeals to her sometimes. And Unitarian belief would at least solve the problem of Christ, she thinks. Miriam has learned enough about theologies and churches merely to intensify an old problem:

Making up your mind that God is to be found only in humanity is humanism. It was Comte's idea. Perhaps

Unitarians are all Comtists. That is why they dress without style. They are more interested in social reform than the astoundingness of there being people *anywhere*. But to see God everywhere is pantheism. What *is* Christianity? Where are Christians? Evangelicals are humanitarians; rushing about in ulsters. Anglicans know all about the beauty of life and like comfort. But they are snobs and afraid of new ideas. Convents and monasteries stop your mind. But there is a God or a Christ, there is something always there to answer when you turn away to it from everything. (II, 358)

By contrast, there is not this uncertainty in Miriam's critical acuteness toward much of the London world she observes; the desire to know and, by implication, the need to have beliefs, evident in her sentiments about religions, move her to judge with certainty the imperfections of social life. Through her employer, Miriam has met Miss Szigmondy, and together the two women frequently make the rounds of lectures, theaters, concerts, art shows. At one of Miss Szigmondy's "at homes" Miriam observes an "effective" girl, charming to men, and the embodiment of some of her own earlier hopes. Miriam is envious and distrustful of the type:

"Charming girls" were taught to behave effectively, and lived in a brilliant death, dealing death all around them. Nothing could live in their presence. No natural beauty, no spectacle of art, no thought, no music. . . . Yet in social life, nothing seemed to possess any power but their surface animation. (II, 174-75)

Again, during an evening with relatives of Mr. Hancock (her favorite employer), Miriam summarizes in her mind a class of people once respected and envied: "hardworked little textbook people and here and there an enlightened, thwarted man." "The 'lady' was the wife for the profes-sional Englishman—simple, sheltered, domesticated, trained in principles she did not think about, and living by them." (II, 200)

These observations appear to be mature and perceptive as social criticism. And yet one wonders if they represent, in the context of Miriam's general awarenesses in these chap-ters, a clear comprehension of the values by which she seems to judge. There is no rationale for her objections to charming girls or to sham middle-class virtues beyond her impression that a demoralizing falseness pervades many of the groups and individuals she meets. Perhaps, like her quandary about Christianity, when she has ques-tioned the varieties of Christian sects and is still left with her question ("What *is* Christianity?"), her social views, not lacking conviction or astuteness, still beg for their full meaning.

The seeds of a possible answer are growing in an old ferment: Miriam's objection to men. Her employers buy a twelve-volume encyclopedia for the office, and Miriam, in unsuspecting casualness turns to the articles on "Woman." She reads and is inflamed. "There was no getting away from the scientific facts . . . *inferior;* mentally, morally, intellectually, and physically." Science reduces woman, in Miriam's interpretation of the text, to a half-human state, and all because of "Sacred functions . . . highest possibili-ties . . . sacred for what? The hand that rocks the cradle rules the world? The future of the Race? What world? What race? Men." "The wonders of science for women are nothing but gynaecology." (II, 220)

Religion offered no better prospect. "Religion in the world had nothing but insults for women." (II, 222) Miriam begins to equate "maleness" with science, particularly the limitations of scientific fact. It is not science itself which is objectionable to Miriam, but the finality of truthfulness which scientific facts claim to the exclusion of some other orders of fact or truth. To Miriam, something is patently insufficient about science if its truth is the false conception of women in that encyclopedia. In the same way, it is not men that annoy Miriam; it is men's characteristic way of seeing only scientific fact as ultimate truth. Civilization is tainted throughout by maleness rampant.

By inference, the "charming girl" is a victim of male expectation, surrendering her equally valid character to conform to men's ideas of her destiny. The "lady" for the professional husband is equally duped. And here the reader can reasonably shudder at the prospect of intense, quarrelsome Miriam as a militant feminist with a program of redress for wronged womanhood! But fortunately, her enduring concern is broader than programmatic feminist protest.

The significance of *The Tunnel* and *Interim* is most apparent in a scene which allows Miriam to reflect on her several preoccupations, and in such a way as to indicate the advance she has made in her first London years. She attends a lecture on Dante, tolerating the lecture itself, but intently appreciating the reading of some of Dante's poetry. Listening to the "voice of Dante," Miriam is impressed by a "truth"—love as the fundamental moral imperative—which is true because it is self-evident to the individual. This value and its perception through intuition shows the impertinence and the falseness of values not consonant with love and not verifiable by vision. This is a promising perspective for Miriam, the furthest point of development she achieves in these chapters, but it is not a perspective which is totally meaningful to her. The insights occur in the context of Miriam's eager, half-critical pouncing on any and all "truths," for in the Dante reverie she also concludes that post-office savings accounts, betting, gambling, and lotteries are wrong because they produce nothing. Hers is still a highly tentative mind, not yet poised in firmly grounded beliefs.

The Dante reverie continues as Miriam rides the train back to London. The problem of achieving a social—and economic—order, an entire fabric of human relationships, motivated by love is her concern. The means do not occur as clearly as the end, especially if religion be the instrument: "If a man love not his brother whom he hath seen, how shall he love God whom he hath not seen? There was a catch in that like a riddle. Heads I win, tails you lose." (II, 355) "But the turning to the unseen God of love and giving up one's self-will meant being changed in a way one could not control or foresee; dropping everything one had and cherished secretly and having things only in common with other people." (II, 356) Miriam is not prepared for this obliteration of the self; there must be a way to give oneself in love and still retain one's identity as an individual.

The precise meaning of love to Miriam is not entirely clear to the reader, but it is apparently a quality instinctive and quiescent in the individual. Its extension to concerns outside the person, whether to other individuals or society, is at once the acknowledgment of a personal and a social ideal; as spiritual law, its expression may be the inter-related goals of personal fulfillment and social justice. This, it seems, is the dawning awareness which Miriam is beginning to articulate. The paradox of stimulation and recoil at the Wilson menage, her bitter resentment of the "maleness" of science and religion, and her attraction to the potentials of quiescent love do not cohere, because Miriam is not sure how the intuitively sanctioned truth about love can be the answer to Hypo Wilson's scientific, materialist rigidities about life and society, can define and defend the essential value of the feminine character, and can be the technique for realizing the self while one real-izes a social ideal.

Miriam has learned a great many things in *The Tunnel* and *Interim,* diffuse and unfocused as these things some-times appear. Chiefly, she has learned the possibility of comprehending the world in relation to herself without lapsing impatiently into subjective finalities, as was her wont in the earlier chapters. She does not ignore or dismiss the social realities life inevitably presents to her; she makes some effort to understand and judge them through what-ever resources of mind and spirit she has. This advance in her development can be seen in the greater number of illuminations she experiences in "the world" than before. There is the continuing stimulation of natural phenomena: an especially effective experience occurs in the "rose-gold" afterglow of a summer rainstorm. But the "sound" of Shakespeare on the stage can be equally effective; it is after all, like the effect of heightened color in a garden to Miriam. A splendid evening with friends, when she has been stimulated intellectually in conversation, aesthetically by music, brings on the "white white brightness" when, alone, she contemplates the accomplished joy. She attends a lecture at which color slides are shown, and while marveling at the pictures she is aware that the effect of the illuminated colors is the effect of her own sense of bright color "when nothing was there."

All in all, the gap between feeling and perception narrows. Perhaps the title *Interim* suggests a temporary, partial success to be challenged before a greater undertaking in the pilgrimage. *Deadlock,* the title of the next chapter, promises as much.

3

Quite properly, the successive volumes of *Pilgrimage* become increasingly complex. Miriam's consciousness is more and more filled with the cumulative effects of her experiences—intellectual, emotional, and physical. Their accessibility in memory and association is unusually facile, and thus her mind subjects even minor moods and perceptions to a kind of Proustian *approfondissement.* Passing an old woman on Shaftesbury Avenue can be as provocative for Miriam as remembering her first reading of Jevons. The consequent density of *Deadlock, Revolving Lights,* and *The Trap* is itself a measure of the "different" Miriam with whom we must deal.

In these chapters the first clear difference which the reader notices is a more self-assured Miriam. Between *Interim* and *Deadlock* several years pass; Miriam has apparently committed herself to an almost anarchic individualism. There is a contingent cynicism about "civilization" as it implies regulative institutions. Emerson is a favorite author.

The chief agent of Miriam's eventual reining in from her intemperate ideal of the individual is Michael Shatov, a Russian Jew who comes to live at Mrs. Bailey's rooming house and who is immediately attracted to Miriam's intelligence and sensibility. His trained intelligence, a much broader systematic learning than hers, and an incisively critical concern about the human relevance of abstract ideas and systems make Shatov a real challenge to Miriam's excesses. To her uncompromising individualism he offers a corrective by insisting on the reality of the race. To her ecstatic avowal that whatever happens, one can always depend on "spring," Shatov simply remarks, "This appreciation of spring is merely a question of youth."

With him, Miriam attends a series of lectures by Dr. McTaggart, where the arguments against materialist reality which Miriam had been seeking are laid out for her. The remarkable gain for Miriam is the metaphysical necessity to admit that something exists. "Descartes should have said, 'I am aware that there *is* something, therefore I am.'" (III, 171) McTaggart proves to her satisfaction that the spiritual substance which is the self is the only thing that, metaphysically, can be said to exist. The differentiation of selves is infinite, but the universe is a unity of these selves. To Miriam, the effect of this presentation is a kind of deliverance: "You *must* begin with the individual." (III, 171) And, certainly outreaching McTaggart, Miriam concludes later: "Then God is *proved* ..." (III, 172) Michael is sceptical of McTaggart's argument and fears that

Miriam is too easily persuaded of "finalities." He cautions her quietly: "Beware of solipsism."

Miriam has also concluded firmly the supremacy of intuitive truth, and thus it is not surprising that she should find Emerson congenial to her present preoccupations. Not really possessing a temperament for sustained, rigorous metaphysics, Miriam finds in Emerson a similar temperament, and she exults in his poetized program for the divinely individual man. Emerson's rejection of theological orthodoxy doubtless stimulates her, but his mystique of the over-soul and the universal perfection assured by it do not yet trouble her, so grateful is she for all documentation of the sanctity of the individual. And for a time Michael, learning Emerson through Miriam (she teaches him English with Emerson as a text), is impressed—but ultimately by a dim connection between Emerson and his own revolutionist doctrines.

When she is with Michael, Miriam is by no means absorbed always in ideas and books. She is as keenly sensitive to his qualities of personality as she is to his mind. They become affectionate combatants, the reader sensing the first signs of love in Michael even when Miriam seems not to.

With Michael or alone, Miriam relentlessly plays idea against idea, impression against impression, always refining in her own mind the problem of "life" and "truth." Several insights to which she continually returns are crucial in describing this stage of her development. We have noted her commitment to individualism. Assuming the ultimate reality of the spiritual individual (i.e., the psychic being of the person, the nonmaterial existence that is consciousness), Miriam argues that the infinite variety and complexity of human experience has, somehow, to be seen simultaneously in all the wonder and "astonishingness" of its diversity. What the intellect is able to do is merely organize logically what it superficially perceives to be patterns, reductions to basic uniformities. If this is a quality which permits prediction or control of experience, the defect of that quality is its inability to deal with equally "real" experience unaccommodated in the categories of uniformity. This is the objection Miriam has to "deified" science, an objection easily misunderstood as a total rejection of science when it is actually her argument against the sufficiency of science as ultimate truth. If this were not her intent, her point of view would border on an existentialist acknowledgment of the anarchic absurdity of life. But such pessimism is not congenial to Miriam: it is profoundly important to her that there be a way to comprehend life fully and yet avoid the deceptive control characteristic of the masculine intelligence, the logical, categorizing, dogmatizing mind.

The reverberations of these ideas occur oddly sometimes. Mrs. Bailey, her landlady, otherwise not very remarkable, shows a gift for natural insight into personality in her dealings with the boarders, and this observation seems to conclude a line of prior speculations, emerging as an assertion of broad principle:

Justice is a woman; blindfold; seeing from the inside and not led away by appearances; men invent systems of ethics, but they cannot weigh personality; they have no individuality, only conformity or nonconformity to abstract systems. (III, 37)

Another kind of reverberation is apparent when Miriam takes Michael to the British Museum for the first time and, stimulated by his presence and by his usual challenges, she is briefly disturbed because her heretofore privately satisfying visits are changed by this presence. She reflects:

The chill of Mr. Shatov's indifferent response to her explanation was buried in her private acknowledgment that it was he who had forced her to discover something of the reason of her enchantment. He forced her to think. She reflected that solitude was too easy. It was necessary, for certainties. Nothing could be known except in solitude. But the struggle to communicate certainties gave them new life; even if the explanation were only a small piece of the truth. (III, 62, 63)

The reader is not only conscious here of the characteristic method of Miriam's mind in adjusting beliefs as new experience modifies them, but also of the valuating "feeling" —later to emerge as the "feminine consciousness"—that doubts the adequacy even of language to deal with the certainties arising in solitary contemplation.

Again, in a more involved sequence, the assimilation of observations and thoughts brings belief. Miriam walks down a West End street one morning and her mind produces a theory—and judgment—about the people whom the street symbolizes. Most people "were ready to answer questions, showing by their angry defence of their opinions that they were aware, and afraid, of other ways of looking at things. But these society people did not seem to be aware of anything but their one world. Perhaps that was why their social method was not able to hold her for long together." (III, 241)

The single world these people see is, to them, so unquestion-
able that there is no room for questions. Nothing can be
communicated except the latest news; and scandal; information about people who have gone outside the shape. But, to
each other, even their statements are put in the form of questions. 'Fine day, what?' So that every one may be not ques-
tioned, but questioner. (III, 242)

And yet, Miriam is fascinated by the genuine elite, who
"disarmed attack, because in their singleness of nature
they were not aware of anything to defend." "They had
no contempts, not being specially intellectual; and credit-
ing every one with their own condition, they reached to the
sources of nobility in all with whom they came in contact."
(III, 242)

Miriam oscillates in these thoughts about West End
people; her mind reaches far back to her ancestry, specu-
lating on the heritage of two "natures" in herself; she is
pointedly aware of the paradox in her desire for the *effect*
of the "charmed life" without its actualities. Thematically,
the episode recalls Miriam's reaction to the Corrie set at
Newlands and points up the difference that has developed
in Miriam since then. Here, she is without the total impatience she felt with the Corries; here, she reflects an intellectual position involving the conflict in her mind
between what she calls the masculine and feminine perspectives. For, after all, to Miriam the West End life is
partial, unilateral, leaving unacknowledged (or at least
unassimilated) the obvious reality of multiple varieties of
life, all meaningful to the genuinely feminine consciousness which sees the wholeness of things.

With such a belief in an all-inclusive faculty of perception, Miriam gets involved in contradictions of which she is both cognizant and unapologizing: she believes that the feminine genius is to hold all opinions in suspension at once. "It's because they [women] see the relations of things which don't change more than things which are always changing, and mostly the importance to men of the things men believe." (III, 259) The contradictions only trouble her when she thinks of the necessity of somehow reconciling beliefs or committing herself to a single point of view which would give positive, assertive direction to her life. There is a fundamental deadlock for her.

The choices between solitude and society, spiritual and physical satisfactions, different modes of conduct is not so simple as it seemed at Banbury Park or Newlands. Hence, the possible choices appear as lights, none entirely constant or direction-giving, but all revolving, beckoning her by turns, with Miriam figuratively unmoving as she contemplates their circular succession. Her defensive concern for "misunderstood" or unfairly treated womankind demands at times a program, but when the feminist organization is suggested to her, she rejects it by exclaiming: "Feminists are not only an insult to womanhood. They are a libel on the universe." (III, 219) The chaos which men feel bound to overcome in the name of civilization and of which women are supposed to be a prime example is the principal masculine illusion, she argues. There never was that kind of chaos. Women exemplify the higher ordering of experience, of which masculine-minded men are incapable. The feminists want to prove women's equality by proving themselves masculine-minded. A dimly visible light, bright for Miriam but not adequately illuminating.

With Hypo Wilson, Miriam feels a closer and closer sympathy, despite his overbearing masculine egotism. He kindles still another light: a program of "specialized action" which would complement her solitary concern for an improved society. Hypo is a leader of the Lycurgan (Fabian?) socialists and persuades Miriam to a "clear theory of the working of the whole of human life." (III, 252) But the lights revolve and Miriam hesitates between the satisfaction of an interior awareness of the rightness of socialist theory, momentarily expressed in an understanding presence, and the dubious value of her participation in the Lycurgan group. She does become a Lycurgan, but in time this light too recedes and Miriam's inveterate individualism forces judgment. To Hypo she declares: "And you know when I hear all these convincing socialists planning things that really would make the world more comfortable, they always in the end seem ignorant of humanity. . . . It's *individuals* who must change, one by one." (III, 374) And ultimately: "The Lycurgans are not humanitarians. Because they are humanitarians deliberately. Liberals and socialists are humanitarians intellectually, through anger. Humanitarian idealists." (III, 379)

It is not surprising that in her rapid turning here and there intellectually, Miriam should relax less and less in the mysterious absorptions of her illuminations. Miriam is still aware that the "something" of those moments lies quiescent in her. At a picnic, on a bicycling trip through the countryside, at the seashore on holidays with her sisters—there are occasions when the "something" wells up within to give joy and peace. But under the rigors of her London life and the complexities of her interests there is an agonizing discrepancy between that feeling and the actualities of living. Sometimes the two seem to converge temporarily as in her double view of socialism which, passively, is an ideal sanctioned by "vision" and, actively, a program of reform. But they do not cohere. It is as though, in trying to harmonize feeling and perception, she succeeded in misplacing the feeling more disappointingly than ever.

They do cohere in perhaps the most dramatic episode of these chapters. In Miriam's first kiss from Michael the unity of inner and outer, spiritual and physical, self and other is momentarily realized. Miriam was aware of her growing emotional involvement with Michael; she was more acutely aware of his undisguised love for her. As usual, she is beset by alternative interpretations of their relationship: it pleased her that he found her intellectually stimulating; it pleased her equally that a mutely continuing desire to be admired as a woman, to entertain prospects of marriage and a conventional destiny as a woman seemed possible through Michael. In their first kiss Miriam is ecstatic, feeling a "wealth within herself now being strangely quarried." (III, 192) "She was at last, in person, on a known highway, as others, knowing truth alive." (III, 192) The sign of light, always integral in her illuminations, here becomes darting flame; "the gold of the sunlight, the magic shifting gleam that had lain always day and night, year-long in tranquil moments upon every visible and imagined thing, came at last into her very hold. It *had* been love then, all along. Love was the secret of things." (III, 194-95)

This was love; marriage was another matter, involving views of life: she and Michael disagreed too finally about that. He would expect the Jewess' domesticity. And what of their religions? Marriage, like religion, was suspicious insofar as it formulated a role for "swaddling women up." After much soul-searching, thought, and argument she tells Michael that she is convinced she will never marry anyone. Michael's answer provokes an unuttered response that thematically illustrates the disjuncture of certainty characterizing these "revolving lights" episodes:

"You think you will never marry . . . with *this*"—his ungloved hand moved gently over the outlines of her shoulders. "Ah—it is most—musical; you do not know." She thrilled to the impersonal acclamation; yet another of his many defiant tributes to her forgotten material self; always lapsing from her mind, never coming to her aid when she was lost in envious admiration of women she could not like. Yet they contained an impossible idea; the idea of a man being consciously attracted and won by universal physiological facts rather than by individuals themselves. (III, 303)

A rigorous individualism indeed. But the profound reality of the love experience, now known, has moved Miriam considerably forward.

Toward the end of *Revolving Lights* two feelings begin to crystallize, foreshadowing a focus for Miriam. She had begun to feel, in the midst of all the variously demanding experiences, that "she must go on, uselessly, unrevealed; bearing a semblance that was nothing but a screen set up, hiding what she was in the depths of her being." (III, 289) Later, through memory, the experience of her first attendance at a Quaker meeting recurs and casts "a soft grey light within the darkness concealing the future." (III, 324) The recollection is pointed. At the meeting she was gratified to see at last people who understood silence; people who knew alone and in congregation a shared religious life impartial to the sexes; a way of life which acknowledged that "being in the silence was being in something alive and positive; at the center of existence; being there with others made the sense of it stronger than when it was experienced alone." (III, 327) The women were equally and fully a part of the enterprise; they, in fact, were more clearly possessed of the inner life of the meeting than the men. "They looked enviably, deeply, richly alive, on the very edge of the present, representing their faith in their persons, entirely self-centred and self-controlled; poised and serene and withdrawn, yet not withholding. . . . Their dignity was not dignified." (III, 329)

The continuing influence of McTaggart's philosophy leads Miriam to reflect on the similarity to Quaker thought of its idealist conception of human existence. But he insisted on the absurdity of pure being, accounting for no substance superior to the individual, neither a metaphysical absolute nor a religious God. Miriam hesitates, groping in her mind for assurance that there must be a pure being— God?—inhabiting the silent individual and binding all individuals in a unity beyond themselves. (Cf. III, 327-30) But she is not sure of this. She can share with the Quakers thoughts on the dichotomy between an intellectual system and a "felt" experience, though to Miriam it is still a dilemma needing resolution.

The other, less promising focus concerns Hypo. The reader is aware that Miriam's relationship with Michael Shatov, failing in its course through love, is subtly transferred to Hypo, at whose home Miriam spends more and more time. With Hypo Miriam seems to be at her fullest competence; their talks and debates range widely over politics, war, socialism, art, sex. As if to foreshadow later developments, Miriam admits to herself that her access to Hypo's mind is not unmixed with pleasure at access to his great charm as a man; Hypo is not unaware of, nor embarrassed to acknowledge Miriam's physical attractiveness to him. He frankly but cautiously courts her intimacy. Miriam is poised again for the love experience.

It does not come immediately, though in *The Trap* there is a marginal attention—intimate, expectant—to Hypo in Miriam's consciousness. *The Trap* is brief; some time has passed since *Revolving Lights;* the interlude has quieted Miriam considerably. There is a somber, brooding atmosphere in sharp contrast to the intensities of *Deadlock* and *Revolving Lights.* To economize, Miriam has taken a small flat with a Miss Holland in Flaxman Court. (We never find out the particular circumstances of her move from the Bailey house, nor of her acquaintance with Selina Holland.) She is twenty-eight now, and suffering a kind of emotional fatigue; she is often alone and in her solitary contemplations seems immobilized by the jarring elements of her life so far. At a young women's club she gives a small dinner party for Michael, the Taylors (friends from the early Lycurgan, "intellectual," radical days) and Dr. Densley (familiar in the past as the humane traditionalist, absorbed in the best values of the elite world, tolerant of her "advanced" views and life, and hopeful that she will eventually attain, by marrying him, her destined womanhood, for which "he was ready to become the gay priest of initiation into the comedy whose every dramatic possibility he knew by heart." [III, 477]). At this dinner party she is oppressed by realizing that "in bringing together three of her worlds [it had] shown her more clearly than she had known it before, that there was no place for her in any one of them." (III, 474)

The essence of Miriam's defeatist mood is a striking admission which, in respect to a great deal she has fought out with herself previously, profoundly suggests the desperation and futility in which she is trapped:

The old life and death struggle between conflicting ideas had died down. She could see the self who had lived so long upon that battleground, far off; annoying, when thought of as suffered by others. But it was not without a pang that she looked back at that retiring figure. It had been, at least, with all its blindness, desperately sincere. She was growing worldly now, capable of concealments in the interest of social joys, worse, capable of assumed cynicism for the sake of advertising her readiness for larks she was not quite sure of wishing to share. And thought was still there, a guilty secret, quiet as a rule. Sometimes inconveniently obtrusive at moments when she most wished to approximate to the approved pattern of charming femininity. (III, 482)

Densley offered marriage—so did Michael—but "marriage is no solution, only a postponement." (III, 482) She would be no nearer her quest for identity through a sense of reality. "She was ready now to drop all props and wander forth. Lo here, lo there. But the kingdom of heaven is within. . . . Yet the kingdom within is a little grey and lonely." (III, 482) And there remained the triple tangle of sex, religion, and art.

Sex implies marriage. Marriage is objectionable on principle—the kind of marriage men require. But celibates, outside religion, are a little absurd, socially; and though "free-lovers seem all in some indefinable way shoddy. . . . free-love is better than absurdity." (III, 495)

To which dilemma is added a brief, poignant reflection on religion:

Strangeness of the seaside at Christmas time. Sunlit frost on the morning grass. Green garden in full sunlight. Blaze of blue sea and blue transparent sky. Blue and green and gold of summer, and warmth in the tingling air. All the things of an old-fashioned Christmas except religion. Deliberate Christmasing, without belief. (III, 505)

The symbol of the problem of art is W. B. Yeats, who lives in a flat across the street from Miriam's and sits in his window giving no thought to the

. . . rampant multitudes. . . . Yet they threatened him as he sat there. Made his joy small and absurd. . . . But he was aware only of his poetry and the sounding board, the green-robed woman sitting low in the opposite chair. . . . She saw him . . . the halting half man's half woman's adoration he gave to the world he saw, his only reality.

And while she admired, she pitied.

And fifty yards away the toilers raged. (III, 502)

This is not a plea that art be sociological, serving the causes of the rampant multitudes. It is Miriam's conviction that art should be a vision of the reality of life directly encountered, not, as she understood him, Yeats's divorce of art and life in his "only reality" of esoteric withdrawal.

Losing hope about the possibility of a knowledge of reality, at least as she has pursued it thus far, Miriam therefore is unsure of how sex ought to be regarded in a contemplated affair with Hypo. Lacking too a religious conviction, and unsure of the substance of the writing career she hopes for, Miriam feels trapped in a corner with death. "But it is I who am left, and not dead." It is the essential self that is left. That self and an unimpaired will assured the "single knowledge that she was going away from this corner where she had been dying by inches. No consideration of right or wrong. No feeling for persons. . . . I must create my life. . . . Self and circumstances the raw material." (III, 508) In the midst of these resolutions, the horrifying screams of the downstairs tenants fighting, threatening each other's lives, then sobbing bitterly in tender remorse, rouse Miriam. With the embattled Mrs. Perrance she feels a profound sympathy, for Mrs. Perrance is "sobbing in serene despair. Without fear." (III, 509)

We cannot speak of the climax or climactic episode in *Pilgrimage;* its content is not conceived in terms of a dramatic development of successive actions. It is possible to speak only of a critical point or state of mind in the emergence of the consciousness defining Miriam Henderson. We recall that Miss Richardson deplored the "dramatic" novelist because he ignored the "unique modifications of contingency" in his selection of experiences for climactic effects or essayistic purposes. The summary analyses in this chapter are meant to show what seem to be the major modifications effected in Miriam's consciousness as she reacts to a great flux of experiences. From *Pointed Roofs* through *The Trap* the central disposition in Miriam's consciousness has been a transcendental individualism variously buffeted and variously justified, but ultimately contiguous to a philosophical idealism akin to that of J. M. E. McTaggart, to whose thought Miriam alludes approvingly several times. It is his particular idealism that defines intellectually to Miriam the rightness of her individualism and, for example, her feeling about the sterility of Lycurgan socialism. McTaggart argued that the fundamental uniqueness and independent reality of every self did not necessitate the absolute isolation of the individual, but rather that there was a vital relation between persons achievable only in love, a quality inherent in the self and impossible to be "brought about" except through the will of the persons. It must express itself in a mystically achieved harmony of selves in a selfless communion.[7] To Miriam, the volitional movement of one's whole being in a fundamentally self-conscious and yet selfless harmony with humanity was not achieved in socialist reform activities: love is not the essence of economics or politics.

The philosophical idealism which thus informed Miriam's perception is a rigorously intellectual system (except for the mystique of love) requiring the logical analysis, interpretation, and statement which are the essence of that masculine intelligence she wars against so vehemently. Miriam champions the higher order of intuitive perceptions, but the masculine part of her own intelligence seeks certainty in the systems she distrusts. The paradox suggests her lack of confidence in the sufficiency of the feminine consciousness, but it also suggests her dissatisfaction with the insufficiency of intellectual systems.

This dilemma is a major modification in her consciousness, which ultimately affects her partial commitment to philosophical idealism, for the conclusion of its logic is that there can be no substance or being superior to the finite individual except an absolute which, according to McTaggart, is virtually incomprehensible and thus approximates Nothing.[8] "Dr M'Taggart said pure being was nothing. But there is no such thing as nothing," (III, 327) is Miriam's frustration with her idealism. The sense of something that mattered beyond finite persons is present still in Miriam. McTaggart's "love" could recommend itself as the something, either in its form as Michael's love or as the ideal she first sought in socialism. But she is concerned about a cause and a suprapersonal object. The thought of God may make life embarrassing, she says, but "the thought of no God made life simply silly." (III, 173)

Miriam's dissatisfaction with philosophical idealism is largely her uncertainty about the nature of being and the nature of God or an Absolute as such a system defines them. Because of this uncertainty, there frequently looms before Miriam an immensity called "life": the wholeness or unity behind disjunctive appearances or "living." The flux of experience needs the masculine genius to formulate external existence into manageable concepts and laws which make living orderly and predictable, but these provide no access to life. The feminine genius is to see behind the façade of the flux. But the abstraction "life" seems arid, as arid and remote as an idealist absolute. Here, it is possible to think of Miriam as having verged on the Bergsonian perspective. The distinction she draws between the feminine and masculine consciousnesses may appear to parallel Bergson's distinction between intuition and intellect. But Bergson's intuition is informed, predicated on an assimilation of prior discursive processes, and thus opposed to intuition as a way of knowing entirely independent of discursive thought and analysis—the kind of intuition Miriam ascribes to the feminine mind. Moreover, Bergson conceived of reality in terms of dynamic creativity and motion; it is repeatedly apparent to Miriam that her only moments of a sense of reality are in silent, contemplative stasis, alive to being, not to Bergsonian becoming. The difference expresses itself obliquely in Miriam's rejection of Densley for his "incomplete conception of life. Every symbol he used called up the image of life as process, never in any direction as completeness." (III, 476)

Miriam has come up against so many seemingly insoluble dilemmas in her quest for harmony and unity of the self in a sense of reality that she is intellectually frustrated and emotionally fatigued. She surveys her life with frank dismay, but not without hope and determination. And not without an unmodified self—the self she long ago called her "nearest most intimate self." One clear possibility for attaining its apotheosis remains: mysticism.

4

The fact of mysticism as a state of consciousness, an operable life view, or as a speculative tendency in philosophy requires no new proof. William James applied the resources of empirical psychology to mysticism and concluded:

. . . the existence of mystical states absolutely overthrows the pretension of non-mystical states to be the sole and ulti-mate dictators of what we may believe. As a rule, mystical states merely add a supersensuous meaning to the ordinary outward data of consciousness. They are excitements like the emotions of love or ambition, gifts to our spirit by means of which facts already objectively before us fall into a new ex-pressiveness and make a new connection with our active life. . . . It is the rationalistic critic who plays the part of denier in the controversy, and his denials have no strength, for there never can be a state of facts to which new meaning may not truthfully be added, provided the mind ascend to a more enveloping point of view.[9]

And, conveniently, J. M. E. McTaggart, a professional philosopher, at the conclusion of a rigorously logical essay on "The Further Determination of the Absolute," defends mysticism as such an enveloping point of view—however difficult it may be to accept:

It would be useless to attempt to deny that the conclusions I have endeavoured to support are hopelessly mystical. In admitting this I shall be thought by many people to have pro-nounced their condemnation. But mysticism is not so easily to be got rid of. The attempt to join in a vital unity things which the consciousness of everyday life regards as separate —and this is mysticism—is inherent in philosophy, which can neither disregard the difference, nor be contented without the unity.[10]

It is possible, thus, to define mysticism as a belief in a unity of the universe impossible to know through ordinary perception or by means of discursive, rational processes alone, and as a belief in the possibility of the human perception (and the attainment) of that unity through supersensuous, nonrational processes. These are the fundamental beliefs underlying the varieties of religious mysticism and the even greater varieties of individual mystics. The various refinements of mysticism in Eastern and Western religions, in nonreligious metaphysical speculation, and among individuals in particular religions are a complex scheme to study. Our concern will be with a particular kind of mystical experience, and more importantly, the kind of consciousness through which it is possible and for which there is a definable process of development.

In one of the most comprehensive modern studies of mysticism,[11] Evelyn Underhill distinguishes mysticism as a quest for reality which, in religious terms, promises "the perfect consummation of the Love of God," or in nonreligious terms, the "establishing [of a] conscious relation with the Absolute."[12] It affords an achievement of reality which is impossible in what Miss Underhill calls "the great classic theories concerning the nature of reality." She examines philosophic naturalism, idealism, and scepticism, and though carefully acknowledging them to answer in part some of man's abiding questions about himself and his world, she finally argues that they leave unsatisfied the quest for reality: naturalism, by offering only a symbolic world of appearance as real; idealism, by merely describing an attractive spiritual absolute which it leaves unattainable; and scepticism, by relying on "pure reason" and denying a knowable or logically conceivable transcendent, and thus necessitating pragmatic truths bordering, in extreme cases, on nihilism.[13] A further theory, called vitalism and illustrated in Bergson and

Rudolph Eucken, has the merit of being able "to accept and transfigure the statements of physical science . . . leave place for those ontological speculations which seem to take their rise in psychology . . . [to provide] an important place for moral and spiritual activity in the universe . . . [and] of involving not a mere diagram of metaphysical possibilities but a genuine theory of knowledge."[14] Its primary difference from the classic schools is that its focal point is not a stable Being, but a fluid Becoming. It would thus be a satisfying theory, except that the deep instinct of the human mind insists not only on a unity of being, but on a "permanent adjustment of his being to the greater life of reality"; he is not content with the fragmentary, momentary perception of the real suggested in Bergson's concept of the cinematographic intellect.[15] This is Miss Underhill's charter for mystical experience. Its achievement is not simply a sudden, mysterious access to truth; it is rather an ordered, temporized development of consciousness "entailing . . . the liberation of a new, or rather latent, form of consciousness."[16] The developmental process is the historic Mystic Way.

Miss Underhill's definition of the Mystic Way—self-awakening, purification, illumination, the "dark night of the soul," and the unitive state—is based on the experiences of the great historical mystics, but she interprets the process in terms of modern psychological thought. She is also committed to the belief that the term of mystical development is a unitive state vouchsafed to the few who by temperament, grace, and diligence can attain it. This is a part of the Catholic framework of her study and is, of course, not totally acceptable to its polar theological

opposites, e.g., Quakerism. Rufus Jones distinguishes two
kinds of mystics: negation mystics, whose single aim is to
experience the union with God, becoming thus one with
infinity and negating self and all finitude; and affirmation
mystics, whose desire is that "vision" should be the beginning, rather than the end, of the mystic's quest, service
and action being the values concomitant to achieving an
immediate experience of God, which will illuminate the
finite self rather than obliterate it.[17] Miss Underhill's
negation mysticism does not invalidate, for the Quaker
mystic, her analysis of the developmental process of the
mystical consciousness. If we adjust, then, her analysis to
the simpler Quaker belief in affirmation mysticism and
with it the Quaker position that the experience is not a
gift of grace to a few, but possible to every man by virtue
of his partaking of the spirit of God in himself,[18] we will
be able to discuss the final phase of Miriam Henderson's
development in *Pilgrimage.*

This discussion of ideas and beliefs should not suggest
their easy application to *Pilgrimage,* as though it were an
exercise in philosophical disquisition. Nor does Miriam
make a deliberate, mechanical study of each in turn, as
though she were shopping for a comfortable philosophy.
Rather, we are concerned to interpret the patterns of her
conscious responses in terms of familiar, generalized perspectives which describe, even tangentially, the character
of her perception and assimilation of experience. Assumptions, inferences, even propositions are involved in Miriam's reactions and these are analyzable in the terms suggested here.

By the end of *The Trap,* Miriam has developed a perspective—or lack of one—resembling Miss Underhill's "charter" for mysticism. The inadequate scientific realism, imperfect idealism, and abortive Bergsonian vitalism leave her still in quest of reality. Miriam is psychologically prone to feelings of transcendence; she yearns for a satisfying idea *and* experience of God; she seeks a social and moral ideal which fulfills the individual and assures social organization; she prefers the feminine consciousness—intuitive, synthesizing, comprehensive. All of these dispose Miriam toward the solutions of mysticism.

The first phase of a developing mystical consciousness is self-awakening, a kind of conversion entailing the "abrupt or gradual emergence of intuitions from below the threshold, the consequent re-making of the field of consciousness, an alteration in the self's attitude to the world."[19] If the process is gradual, there will be intermittent intuitions tending to objectify a sense of reality—a feeling of beyond paralleled or accompanied by heightened sense impression—as a place or person or condition of being. Visible nature can be important to the subject as exhibiting the divine in nature or as having a different beauty, a "glory" after or during the momentary intuition. There will also be a pattern of vision and reaction as the intuitions of the spiritual consciousness (to some writers, the subconscious or subliminal) alternate with the cognitions of the superficial consciousness in the subject's finite life. The recurrent intuitions in the gradual awakening give greater and greater lucidity—though almost imperceptibly changing, perhaps—and may begin at any age or endure to any length in the life of the subject.[20]

The parallel between this process and the pattern of

Miriam's development through *The Trap* may be inferred without itemizing again their particulars. But there is not, at the end of *The Trap,* the characteristic effect of conversion or awakening; there have been "storm and stress, the vague cravings and oscillations," but the altered perspective of release into a "larger world of being" is missing. In the next chapter, *Oberland,* that effect, as Miss Richardson conceives it for Miriam's life, is accomplished.

Oberland is brief, joyous, lyrical. Seeking respite from the mood of *The Trap,* Miriam is on holiday in the Swiss Alps. The joy of being in the midst of the sublime beauty of the towering mountains and in the cold, clear air recalls her chief happiness of the past and gives her a sustained feeling of spiritual buoyancy. The light on the mountains stirs her: "It was as if all her life she had travelled towards this radiance and was now within it, clear of the past, at an ultimate destination." (IV, 49) The mountains and immense landscape "invited thoughtless submission to their influence as to a final infinite good that would remain when they were no more seen." (IV, 72) Tobogganing, she feels a sense of release from the earth, a "flight into paradise," so exhilarating is the atmosphere and experience. (IV, 74) Ice-skating was "Gliding, as if forever; the feeling, coming even with the first uncertain balance, of breaking through into an eternal way of being." (IV, 87) The "unexpressible" feeling registers for her—and is communicated by Dorothy Richardson—in images of space-time transcendence.

The best moments of good feeling are solitary and the "world" seems diminished, "the delicious sense of known worlds waiting far below [she is hiking up a mountain],

world behind world in a chain whose end was the far-off
London she represented here in this high remoteness. . . ."
(IV, 101) But the enchantment pervades her social experiences as well. She is her usual observant self in the
midst of the rituals of hotel social life, but she is not her
usual caustic self. Two young men at the hotel are frequently with her, but she lapses only once into her inveterate denunciation of characteristic men, and then softly.
Most of the Oberland people, despite their surface
crotchets, have an "unfaltering aspect," singleness, personality. She thinks of London:

For the first time, she was seeing London as people whose
secret had revealed itself during this last two weeks, and was
at this moment beginning consistently to live her life there
as in future it would be lived, as she had lived it, but unconsciously and only intermittently, during the past year.
(IV, 123)

Hypo is in that life; Miriam is thrilled by his professed
love for her; he has been, however, a shadow on that life
who might, in love, become its sunshine.

The source of Miriam's Oberland joy is, in the mystic's
language, "the revelation of an external splendour, the
shining vision of the transcendent spiritual world."[21] The
joy itself is the mark of an accomplished awakening if
there accompanies it its necessary complement: crystalliza-
tion, participation, a "personal" and imperative concept
that shows itself in changed behavior and attitudes.[22]
Miriam in *Oberland,* particularly her resolution to "live
in its effect" in future, has experienced her awakening,
her "release."

The title of the tenth chapter of *Pilgrimage—Dawn's Left Hand*—suggests its scope: the first, tentative emergence of the "new" Miriam. The effect of the Oberland experience is evident in Miriam's first renewals of her London life. She finds her old north London friends, seen infrequently since Wordsworth House days, newly valuable. Flaxman's is unchanged—the garbage and stench and general decay are there—but the golden glow of Oberland sustains her. She sees Densley again, and momentarily wishes to accept his renewed offer of marriage. She hesitates, he misinterprets her hesitation as offense, and she concludes it is just as well, since the "visible pageant of marriage," a floral wedding, rose before her eyes, not the "newness of life" into which she might gladly enter. (IV, 154-55)

With Hypo her feelings are mixed. He was in love in his way, a way promising little to her "inner being," simply because "his brilliance, the mental qualities she had hitherto found so full of charm, had somehow, unaccountably, become overshadowed." (IV, 141-42) The person with whom Hypo would now have to deal was the continuous person who at six years old was enchanted upon the garden path, and, rediscovered at Oberland, was "now going, deceitfully, to local, social Lycurgan meetings, frequenting them, since Oberland, only for small delights that were the prelude, the practice-ground for more and more." (IV, 177-78)

They become lovers—but not successfully. The major part of *Dawn's Left Hand* is concerned with the remarkable travails of Miriam in love and sex. Before the affair has progressed very far, Miriam begins to sense its failure

—and to see the reasons for it. Hypo "was incapable of homage," and there was a woman, "not this thinking self who talked to men in their own language, but one whose words could be spoken only from the heart's knowledge, waiting to be born in her." "It was his constricted, biological way of seeing sex that kept him blind. Beauty, even, was to him beauty by contrast with Neanderthal man." (IV, 230-31) The affair left her spiritual being unattained. During one tryst she tells him of an experience in extra-sensory perception she has had, and is encouraged by his reply that "One has these curious premonitions in certain moods. Certain states of heightened perception. One is exalted and luminous." (IV, 228) But he is unwilling to grant any ultimacy to it. Realizing this separateness for them even in the intimacy of their tryst, Miriam answers with a surprising statement which she does not develop: "Art, sex, and religion; one and the same."

The "triple tangle" occurring to her in this context may be a reflex to Hypo's inveterate scientific scepticism, which would apply equally to art, sex, and religion. In any case, sex is its own end to the sentient being, an attitude agreeable to Hypo the scientific liberal. But Miriam, characteristically ignoring any orthodox religioethical restriction of sex to procreation, wants to regard sex in its spiritual character, perhaps its sacramental function, achieving the "exalted" and "luminous" self. Only thus, in her current commitment to Oberland, would the reality of sex be certain. To distract one's innermost self in the face of the sensual experience is an extraordinary achievement for Miriam, signifying a detachment worthy of its mystical meaning. On a visit to Hypo and Alma Wilson, Miriam goes early to bed one night. Hypo comes unexpected to her room, and though allowing his attempts at love-making, Miriam is able to preserve her self from involvement in the experience.

It was uncanny, but more absorbing than the unwelcome adventure of her body, to be thus hovering, outside and above it in a darkness that obliterated the room and was too vast to be contained by it. . . . [A]fter an instant's sudden descent into her clenched and rigid form, she was now travelling alone on and on, without thought or memory or any emotion save the strangeness of this journeying. (IV, 257)

Just before Hypo came to her room, Miriam had thought: "I'm a free-lover. Of course I'm a free-lover. But not his. On the horizon." (IV, 254)

With modifications for her temperament and circumstances, Miriam is undergoing purification in the mystic's quest. The popular notion of purification is bound up with conceptions of asceticism and denial. But, Miss Underhill explains, the essence of the historic virtues associated with purification—poverty, chastity, obedience—is detachment. Distractions of many kinds—material and immaterial—enslave the self, and hence the process of purification is a gradual but continual assessment of the "illusions" of life and their denial, however painful. For Miriam, too, the pattern of experiences that follow awakening is awareness of the illusion in so many interests and desires she had thought possessed reality. The important thing is attitude; one can be in the midst of luxurious living and yet, by detached valuation of its "unreality," maintain the discipline that is purification.[23] The sex episodes are the central instance of Miriam's purification in *Dawn's Left Hand;* she is glad of her achievement at Bonnycliff (the Wilson home), believing it "had carried her into a way of being that would find its own responses in the dead-seeming world." (IV, 259) The triple tangle is reduced by one.

The process of purification is first detachment and then mortification which, Miss Underhill says, in the language of psychology is the process of setting up new paths of neural discharge. In general terms it is the adjustment of the individual to the demands of the mystic life. Its marks are an unwavering sense of the awakened reality, and an unrelenting contrast between the changing, moving, struggling self in the world of experience, and the stable, eternal *being* present in the intensified feeling of an imminent "beyond." Detachment is the negation of divisive interests and desires; mortification is the positive assertion of the new interests and desires.

It is not possible to mark a point at which one aspect or the other of purification begins or ends in *Dawn's Left Hand;* these chapters blend the two in a dense sequence of experiences that show Miriam negating or affirming their value depending on the extent to which they lend enhancement of the self she now cultivates. An extreme instance of the affirming pattern occurs when Miriam, sitting quietly in a restaurant, is able to provoke the transcendent feeling by deliberate contemplation:

With a single up-swinging movement, she was clear of earth and hanging, suspended and motionless, high in the sky, looking, away to the right, into a far-off pearly-blue distance, that held her eyes, seeming to be in motion within itself: an intense crystalline vibration that seemed to be aware of being enchantedly observed, and even to be amused and to be saying, "Yes, this is my reality." (IV, 279)

The negating pattern is evident in her attitude toward Michael Shatov. They have remained good friends during the years, and in his "persistent helplessness" he has called on her many times for help, advice, encouragement. She has always felt that "whatever hurt him must hurt her also while life lasted." This time, his telegram came and she was undisturbed—sympathetic but undisturbed. She is newly immune to him. She thinks it would be good for him to know Amabel, her latest close woman friend. The introduction effected, she goes with Michael to a concert, and there, both inspired by and oblivious to the music, she confronts her own predicament. Her suspected pregnancy? A brief social embarrassment. More important is "wondering if the whole of the past had been a long journey in a world of illusion," and if she must in the future be removed from the "newly discovered world":

Even now with life stripped bare before her and all its charm departed, wonder, with its question was still persisting. It seemed to call upon her for acceptance, for courage not so much to steel herself against the withdrawal of the old familiar magnetic stream as to push on, in spite of its withdrawal, to the discovery of some new way of being. (IV, 297)

The answer is partly given in Miriam's next encounter with Hypo. She has exorcised their passional life. They talk of life, society, and Miriam's future. Hypo tells her: "I believe you capable of devotion, Miriam. It's one of your attractions. But you evade. And you're a perfectionist, like most young people. But all this admirable young loyalty and singleness of purpose must attach itself somewhere, or fizzle wastefully out." (IV, 331) The counsel is well taken; they talk further and in speaking of modern man's dilemma Hypo warns her that modern life does not readily indulge the "romantic journeys into each other" which Miriam proposes as a satisfactory social method. The solution for Hypo is "running ahead" of impending disaster. "Running where?" Miriam asks. "Away from the wrong life-illusion, Miriam." The answer stings Miriam; she takes it as a rebuke. Her repudiation of Hypo is complete. The residue of the encounter is conviction that there must be a "shape" in surface life for her vision; she does not seek withdrawal.

Later, the same final repudiation of orthodox Christianity and socialism leaves her equally free for the future. Her sister Sarah's illness demands attention; that given, she leaves behind the last vestige of a dying self. She had once said of herself that she always left things to be decided or acted upon on the horizon. The horizon is clear. The clear success of purification is conviction anticipating certainty:

Being versus becoming. Becoming versus being. Look after the being and the becoming will look after itself. Look after the becoming and the being will look after itself? Not so certain. Therefore it is certain that becoming depends upon being. Man carries his bourne within himself and is there already, or he would not even know that he exists. (IV, 362)

The thing lacking is the clear certainty which, for the developing affirmation mystic, is illumination.

Occurring very much as the prior awakening, with the attendant sense of light and emotional rapture, illumination is the accomplishment of a reorientation to life under the conviction that the sense of transcendent reality is clearly a certainty of God immanent in the world of the superficial consciousness and revealing Himself to the contemplative individual. The general awareness of a transcendent spiritual "beyond" achieved in awakening is, in illumination, specifically an awareness of God and the relationship between Him as object and the finite self as subject. To the Quaker, this relationship is the accessibility of the spirit of God in the finite self. Contemplation, the deliberate focusing of attention on the transcendent, is the means of realizing this relationship. Three modes of illumination occur, one or the other characterizing the individual, but sometimes in combination: the sense of the presence of God, the illuminated vision of the world, and psychic upheaval (voices, visions, automatic activity).[24] The third will not concern us; Miriam is not psychologically constituted for that. But the first two are the measure of her illumination, and the achievement of her pilgrimage.

In *Dimple Hill,* the last chapter of *Pilgrimage,* Miriam is taking a long, prescribed rest with a Quaker family in Sussex. The onset of the illuminative experience occurs early in the book when Miriam, sitting quietly on the grass at the Roscorla farm, is reminded of Emerson, the subject of a book she prepares to read. She reflects a while on her changing attitude toward Emerson, remembering her early enthusiasm. She summons an image of him: serene, aloof, enjoying a life of "cultured contemplation," sitting in his library reading and meditating, "with thin, flexible lips firmly set, below keen eyes smiling delighted welcome for a thought-link forming itself within the serenely tumultuous mind." (IV, 418) The image directs her attention to the book she holds; she reads for a moment, then thinks of Emerson again—as thinker, "giver of truth." His thoughts now leave "a haunting shadow . . . of sadness, nostalgia for an essential something missing from Emerson's scheme, whose absence left one alone with serenely burning intellectual luminosities in a universe whose center was forever invisible and inaccessible. Listening within its silence, one heard only his poetic voice, moving from pitch to pitch persuasively, logically, almost relentlessly optimistic." (IV, 420)

The thing missing is the vital presence of God.[25] Seeing a familiar quotation from Emerson in a new context, and mysteriously caught between the thought of Emerson's deficiency and the simple meaning—so elusive—of her own quest, she is startled by the different effect on her of the Emerson lines, an effect which "struck down through her and vanished leaving . . . a physical shock passing through her body." (IV, 420) Suddenly mindful of her physical surroundings again, she sees "upon the upper foliage of a group of trees in the dense mass at the far end of the ridge, a patch of bright colour in a golden light so vivid that for a moment she seemed to discern, as if they were quite near, each of the varnished leaves." (IV, 420)

Risen to her feet, she found the radiant patch more distant and less bright, a small splash of brilliant colour such as she had seen a thousand times before, picked out from a spread

of dark tree-tops by a ray of haze-screened, shadowless sunlight. But the rapture that had seized and filled her emptied
being at the first sight of it still throbbed to and fro between
herself and that far point upon the ridge, and still she felt
the sudden challenge of that near, clear vision, like a signal
calling for response; and like a smile, of amusement over
her surprise.

"I know," she heard herself exclaim towards the outspread
scene whose grey light could no longer deceive. "At last I
know! I have seen the smile of God. Sly smile." (IV, 420)

Though abrupt and amazing to Miriam, the "opening"
is the consequence of the psychological process she has
undergone since her Oberland awakening. Intuitions are
identified with, and confirmed by, God revealing Himself;
feeling and perception are one in Miriam's admission to
that certainty; the mode of her apprehension is both inner
and outer, the heightened feeling within integrating with
the sensuous impression without. This has been the certainty Miriam sought, that her life might be unified in it.
The past, present, and future appear transfigured to her:

Approaching the solitary house, she went quietly. Between
her and the luminous multitude welcoming her from far,
familiar surroundings grown as new and as strange as was
every step of this oft-trodden little pathway, between her and
her man, the unknown sharer of the transfigured earthly life,
quietly going his way amongst those distant friends, there
waited in the battered old house, as within a shrine, the first
of the new, heaven-lit humanity, a part of her own being,
confidently approaching its end. (IV, 421)

The effect of the first mode of illumination—for Miriam the felt presence of God—is continuous, interrupting

in no way the "daily life and mental activities of its possessor; who is not necessarily an ecstatic or an abstracted visionary, remote from the work of the world. It is true that the transcendental consciousness has now become, once for all, his centre of interest; its perceptions and admonitions light up his daily life."[26] As illumination, this experience has shown Miriam that the stable "being" of which she has been aware since childhood and of which she has been reminded intermittently in moments of heightened consciousness is the spirit of God immanent in her as finite person, and thus her reality. The several Miriams she has been in her evolving life in the world are the successive movements of her finite self toward a unity with her infinite, now surely divine self. She has become, in reality, what she is. Its reality illuminated in an achieved mystical vision, the discovered self need no longer be at variance with the illusory selves, here satisfying, there doubtful, which ultimately left reality unknown and un-attained.

The further development of mystical awareness leads to the "term" of the great mystics: the unitive life where, after a lapse into "the dark night of the soul," the mystic experiences an entire obliteration of a sense of self, time, finitude. This is Miss Underhill's term for the mystic's quest, but Rufus Jones, assessing the Catholic conception of mysticism from the point of view of Quaker, affirma-tion mysticism, contends:

That undoubtedly is the classical use of the word "mystical." . . . The great mystics of history who have claimed to have had this ecstatic experience, have thought of it as a super-natural gift of divine grace and have felt a peculiar exaltation of spirit as a result of it, but it is quite obvious that mystical experiences of that type could furnish no content of thought. Those who have had the experience are convinced by it that God is *real,* are certain that they have *found* Him, and that they have been caught up into union with Him, but they cannot hint to human ears any descriptive circumstances about the actual character of God.[27]

It was doubtless with such an attitude toward Miriam's mystical awareness that Dorothy Richardson developed its particular character in the environment of a Quaker household. The first of the new "heaven-lit humanity" are the Roscorlas, with whom she boards. To Miriam, the value of living in communion with a vital reality is symbolized in this Quaker family. Their reality is the representation of the "character of God," known in contemplation of the Inner Light, in their single lives, in their social perspective, in their attitude toward the world of nature and of practical affairs. It is clear in *Dimple Hill* that Miriam has not identified herself with the Friends as a sectarian creed or church. Passing by a "chapel" church, Miriam is reminded that: "the depths of her nature had been subtly moulded long ago by its manifold operations and could never fully belong to the household on the hill." (IV, 451) But the Quaker way of life is, symbolically, "the illuminated vision of the world":

Here, amongst the Roscorlas the sense of everlastingness is about one all the time. And the sense of indestructible individuality. (IV, 515)

Certain of the reality within as the spirit of God, the Quakers' method—contemplation— is feminine because it is intuitive, transcendent; hence, they are able to see all in terms of a stable one, or the finitely complex and contradictory in terms of infinite unity and harmony under the aspect of inward truth. Their ideal is love, whether in regard to other single individuals or to social method. To Miriam, as she joyously observes them, the Roscorlas succeed in implementing spiritual ideals in conduct and action.

There are hesitations, of course, and doubts, for Miriam, though "illuminated," is not another Miriam entirely. She simply sees and understands in a way unfamiliar previously. The Quaker belief in arbitration troubles a Miriam accustomed to direct, assertive attack on problems. Attending a Quaker meeting for worship, Miriam earnestly tries to achieve their silent contemplation, but her mind is busy; characteristically, she observes and weighs the method of worship, approving it generally but failing personally in its technique. She wonders, too, about intellectual activity: how much and what kind is compatible with the Quaker mind? An intellectual Friend calls on the Roscorlas and Miriam is relieved to know that Friends do think, but always under the guidance of the Inner Light. She and Mr. Mayne discuss economic theory at dinner, and she is happy that this important concern of hers is not alien to the Quaker pattern she admires.

Under the influence of Dimple Hill life, she begins writing a book, a long-cherished ambition only now possible of fulfillment. Hypo had always encouraged her to write, and with his blessings she had published articles on socialism, but his last advice was that she should write a novel, a "philosophical" novel. Long before, an early suitor had teased her with the idea of writing "the confessions of a modern woman." He had the wrong idea.

She writes, but "there was nothing, in this mass of hurriedly written pages, to justify the havoc-working confession."

They represented a chase, soon grown conscious of its own futility, after something concealed within the impulse that had set her down to write, bringing fatigue and wrath over her failure to materialize it in the narrative whose style was worse than that of the worst books of this kind. . . .

Perhaps if she put it away and forgot it, it might one day be transformable into something alive all over . . . (IV, 524)

The reality of God now known and felt, religion is assured; a novel "alive all over" will be the representation of reality in art. The triple tangle is no more.

Returning from a brief trip to Michael and Amabel's wedding in London—and a chance, reassuring encounter with Hypo—Miriam is conscious of the Roscorlas' apprehension about her and Richard. But she feels the continuing rhythm of her illumination despite the tension:

. . . there is something we all share and that even for me, who am only at the alphabet, is what makes life worth living, the only real culture, the only one that can grow without fading and carry through to the end. (IV, 551)

She longs to stay, but also to leave. Perhaps to Oberland. "Vereker sends, at regular intervals, reminders. Found a new place last winter in Austria. Kitzbühel. Says it leaves Switzerland in the shade and is known, so far, only to a few."

Thus *Pilgrimage* ends, with no finality, but with a sense of the going-on, now differently, of a self realized in the mystic way. Miriam is not the fully developed religious mystic. She has achieved illumination, that of the religious mystic, and also that of the mystic-artist who seeks to communicate his vision of the transcendent reality to his fellows. Miriam's frequent concern in *Pilgrimage* over "something" amiss in the novel form is defined to her when she herself attempts to write one in *Dimple Hill* and finds no adequate convention for her newly certain vision. It is about 1911, and as *Pilgrimage* ends for Miriam Henderson, Dorothy Richardson, novelist, seems imminent.

5

To Miss Richardson, reality is subjective: felt experience is real experience; its modifications of the subject, through perceptions modified by memory and association, are unique to that subject and result in thought formulations and feelings about the "actual" world. We are accustomed to think of this apparatus as the consciousness William James likened to a stream, metaphorically describing its continuity, fluidity, and incremental nature. But, if we recall Miss Richardson's definition of consciousness,[28] we see that she calls the Jamesian consciousness "mind" (in *Pilgrimage*, sometimes the "superficial" consciousness) and perceives beyond this a transempirical self. This self, evident to the person in feelings of transcendence which arise below the level of "mind" and which are independently assertive, is what Miss Richardson regards as consciousness. It is stable because it is eternal *being* rather than the fluid *becoming* which is the "superficial" consciousness. It is these ideas which underlie her belief in "the originality of life at all levels."[29] The reality of God no less than the reality of a door is its felt presence in the subject. This, ideologically, is Miss Richardson's "feminine reality."

Since experience is not real except as it becomes felt life in a subject, the nature of life as the activity of the superficial consciousness and the activity of stable consciousness poses the problem of their adjustment for the subject's sense of his real identity. Minimizing or denying a transempirical self and believing one's reality to be identical with the superficial consciousness is a possible adjustment, typically masculine; doubting the sufficiency of the superficial consciousness and being able to accommodate its activity to that of intuitions from the stable consciousness is another adjustment, typically feminine— and better, according to Miss Richardson. "[T]he unique gift of the feminine psyche, available as long as her mind is not warped from its own 'shapeless' shapeliness [is] its power to do what the shapely mentalities of men appear incapable of doing for themselves, to act as a focus for divergent points of view." "Ceaselessly within her is a small gleam of the infinity men seek to catch within the shapes of systems of religion, of philosophy, and of science."[30] Self-realization, achievement of personality, is harmonizing the two elements in the individual—what, Miss Richardson agrees, is meant by harmonizing Dr. Jung's division of the self into *persona* and *anima*, "the one turned towards objects, centrifugal, and the other towards inner experience, centripetal."[31] For her, the more inclusive harmony is the *anima*-feminine. This is Miss Richardson's "feminism," which, inextricably connected with the psychological development of Miriam, is the thematic structure unifying *Pilgrimage*.

CHAPTER III

The Tapestry Hangs Complete

REALITY, MIRIAM LEARNS, is known within when one contemplates there the universal, timeless spirit that is one's stable self. The psychology of quietism, the significance of this contemplation, Dorothy Richardson says, is that:

When awareness is concentrated on one thing, all else fades away to the margin of consciousness. The "thing" which has had the power of so arresting us, of making a breach in the normal, unnoticed rhythm of the senses, allows our "real self" —our larger and deeper being, to which so many names have been given—to flow up and flood the whole field of the surface intelligence. . . .[1]

Pilgrimage is closely autobiographical. The few facts about herself, particularly about her early life, which Miss Richardson has publicized are the primary facts of Miriam's experiences.[2] When, therefore, after beginning an unsatisfying account of herself, Miriam speaks in *Dimple Hill* of wanting to write a book "alive all over," expressing the "women's side" and including what is always "preceding and accompanying and surviving the drama of human relationships; the reality from which people move away as soon as they closely approach and

expect each other to be all in all," she is Dorothy Richardson saying in her own person that *Pilgrimage* began as a
conventional narrative, but soon there appeared "a stranger
in the form of contemplated reality having for the first
time in her experience its own say."[3]

In her remarks on the psychology of quietistic contemplation, Miss Richardson continues:

> With most of us, beyond these more or less universal ex-
> periences [the experience of beauty on all levels—falling in
> love and "conversion," for example], the times of illumina-
> tion are intermittent, fluctuating, imperfectly accountable, and
> uncontrollable. The "artist" lives to a greater or less degree
> in a perpetual state of illumination, in perpetual communica-
> tion with his larger self. But he remains within the universe
> constructed for him by his senses, whose rhythm he never
> fully transcends. His thoughts are those which the veil of
> sense calls into being, and though that veil for him is woven
> far thinner above the mystery of life than it is for most of
> us, it is there. Imprisoned in beauty, he is content to dwell,
> reporting to his fellows the glory that he sees.[4]

Miriam's falling in love, "conversion," and other experiences of beauty are described in *Pilgrimage;* her report, as
artist, of the glory she sees is Dorothy Richardson's creation of *Pilgrimage.* The mystical consciousness which
Miriam develops is equally the "perpetual state of illumination" Miss Richardson describes for the artist: his
access to reality felt within.

In another place, Dorothy Richardson invokes Wordsworth's definition of poetry—the result of emotion recollected in tranquillity—to explain the essence of psycholog-

ical fiction. Rephrasing Wordsworth's description of the process of recollection, she says:

> . . . the poet, recalling an occurrence that has stirred him to his depths, concentrates thereon the full force of his imaginative consciousness; . . . there presently returns, together with the circumstances of the experience, something of the emotion that accompanied it, and . . . , in virtue of this magnetic stream sustained and deepened by continuous concentration, there comes into being a product this poet names, with scientific accuracy, an "effusion."[5]

The psychological novel is the novel become poetry, she continues, and therefore she speaks of the effusions, not novels, of Marcel Proust and James Joyce, implying their crucial autobiographical genesis and their method of coming into being as art. The speculation applies equally to Miss Richardson if *Pilgrimage* as "independently assertive reality" is the result of plumbing the past to recall the occurrences that stirred Dorothy Richardson "to her depths." The occurrences assert themselves through their force in memory, and the fundamental selection of the matter of Miss Richardson's effusions is accounted for.

Ordinarily, we think of compositional structure in a novel as the selection and arrangement of events that show progression toward some thematic goal. Certain of those events are critical or climactic, exemplifying the important stages of that progression in some sphere of human activity. There may be, for example, simple action (the picaresque novel), psychological enlightenment (Bazarov in *Fathers and Children*), or decisive ethical commitments (Strether in *The Ambassadors*). By various technical devices the novelist can provide an emphatic, discriminatory signal of the meaning which such an event assumes in the total narrative. In this way, compositional structure complements thematic structure; one is the technical means of revealing the other. This relationship between structure and meaning is achieved in psychological fiction by special means; Joyce's "epiphany" or Proust's "privileged moment" replaces the conventional climactic "action." But the moments of "illumination" in Miss Richardson's novel, though somewhat similar as psychic events to epiphany and privileged moment, do not receive this structural emphasis in *Pilgrimage*. Miriam's illuminations are clearly distinguishable from other events in her consciousness, but they are not clearly revelatory of change in her until the ultimate revelation in *Dimple Hill*. And for this reason, in her commitment to imitative realism, Miss Richardson does not divorce the experience from or emphasize it within the context of its occurrence. There is not, therefore, the structural signal in the moment of illumination which one expects in Joyce or Proust. The critical changes in Miriam are essentially broad intellectual and emotional developments diffused from chapter to chapter over the full content of the heroine's consciousness during a wide extent of time. There is no formal structure wherein the conventional accentuation of single critical events provides a pattern. But this is not to say that *Pilgrimage* exhibits no structure whatever.

I

The essential problem of structure in the novel, according to Edwin Muir,[6] is not merely "form" or "pattern" or some other of the familiar concepts we use to describe particular types of structure; it is the organization of the narrative, the arrangement of events with reference to the emphatic use of time or space as the predominating element of control. Thus there are two fundamental types of novel structure: the dramatic novel whose imaginative world is in time, and the character novel whose imaginative world is in space.[7] To these he adds a third type, the chronicle, which extends both time and space limits so far that the relatively stable space and time dimensions, respectively, of the dramatic and character novels are both modified to effect a time-space relationship characterized simply by change.[8] The structure of the chronicle, therefore, is rather completely a time structure, the space mutations being themselves aspects of time. The principle of the structure is process; hence, its point of general reference outside the fiction is not fate as in the dramatic novel, nor society as in the character novel, but life itself, the going-on and change of things generally. Its structure, then, is bound to be the loosest of the three. Muir says further:

Its action is almost accidental, but . . . all the events happen within a perfectly rigid framework. A strict framework, an arbitrary and careless progression; both of these, we shall find, are necessary to the chronicle as an aesthetic form. Without the first it would be shapeless; without the second it would be lifeless. The one gives it its universal, the other its particular reality. As Time, however, is the main ground of the chronicle, so each of those two planes of the plot is a separate aspect of time. They may be called Time as absolute process, and Time as accidental manifestation.[9]

Muir's broad conception of structure does not preclude any number of refinements or technical manipulations in the conception and execution of any novel; it defines the primary problem of any novelist's method. James's point-of-view strategy—or Percy Lubbock's generalization of it —does not stand opposed to Muir's theory; it may be regarded as a particular solution to the basic problems of the dramatic novel. *Pilgrimage* stands in the same relation to Muir's conception of the chronicle, and we can describe the general compositional structure of *Pilgrimage* in such terms. We are dealing with a stream-of-consciousness novel, of course, and we will therefore be concerned with mental events rather than action, and with an "objective, scientific" time and a "subjective, psychological" time.

The external, objective chronology—the uniform, con-secutive, cause-effect series in calendrical time—which ulti-mately bounds any narrative, whether an account of years as in *The Old Wives' Tale* or of a day as in *Ulysses,* is present in *Pilgrimage* as the successive stages of Miriam's achievement of a satisfying sense of her reality. This time control within the quest theme of the novel points up the broadest dimension of its compositional structure as well as the broadest basis of selection in it. If objective, calen-drical time were relevant to *Pilgrimage* only as the book covers a great deal of time in the telling, then we could agree that *Pilgrimage* "arrives at simple chronological sequence" and that "the book does go somewhere—it sets out on the first page and arrives on the last page—but the pages between are mostly detour."[10] But chronological sequence in *Pilgrimage* is not merely that; the sequence is selected and ordered into blocks of time which define the stages of a developing mystical consciousness and provide the objective time framework of the novel. They provide a principle of selection and arrangement as well, a causal, linear structure, organizing groups of experiences around significant states of mind and attitudes and linking them in psychological cause-and-effect relationships. And as these relationships move forward in time toward their final effect (for the heroine) of mystical "illumination," the whole novel is consistently focused in a narrative present which, though often obscure, establishes an objective time control for the events in the separate volumes.

It is, of course, a loose structure; years, not hours or days, are represented. The novel eschews generalized statement for the detailed presentation of the minutiae of consciousness, and hence it is apparent that very little of the eighteen years which elapse between *Pointed Roofs* and *Dimple Hill* can be compassed as the objective present of the narrative; only enough, apparently, to typify Miriam at each of the stages of her growth toward self-realization. *Pointed Roofs,* for example, embraces experiences occurring during a five-month period; *Revolving Lights,* only parts of a few nonconsecutive days; *Oberland,* two weeks. As we shall see later, within the separate volumes we often experience only moments at a time that actually occur during the period the volume represents.

The severe limitation of the actual narrative present to extremely brief, even momentary, periods within the great blocks of time that define the theme is adequate to Miss Richardson's purpose. It allows the narrative to range through the complex vagaries of subjective time only for as long as the moment or moments are sustained and then to be brought back to the linear, causal control of the external structure; a balance of the two levels of time is thus achieved. Where the moments themselves are not reasonably close, there are chapter changes and spacing devices in the separate volumes, as we shall see. But the organization of the volumes around brief objective time cuts provides technically what the theme provides ideologically: an organizing framework for the elaborate detail of Miss Richardson's novel.

But even so limited a scope within the selected periods of development Miriam is shown to undergo would still allow for an unwieldy rendering of the vast contents of consciousness; a rendering of this material needs closer focusing, tighter construction than the objective time structure alone achieves. Unifying the narrative, making it cohere beyond the discipline of theme and external time is the problem. Here, the "far from inconsiderable technical influence" with which Miss Richardson credits Henry James is most apparent. A single mind, Miriam's, is the center of the entire novel. All of setting, characters, action in *Pilgrimage* is presented as Miriam's awareness of them. The range of matter is great; somewhere between the awesome experience of God in a mystical vision and profane embarrassment at the sound of a roommate's use of the chamber pot. But at either extreme, and all between, the matter is an event in a single mind, the quality of which makes possible Miss Richardson's expression of attitudes evaluating the experiences Miriam undergoes and thus projecting the view of life the novel seeks to define.

The identification of heroine's and author's attitudes implied here is important to note. By limiting the point of view thus, Miss Richardson achieves an effect of immediacy, the reader's direct awareness of events in the narrative as they occur. In her view the auctorial detachment achieved by the Jamesian method assures the reader the effect of life observed primarily; this is true because the reality of perceived phenomena is, by definition, their occurrence as events in Miriam's consciousness. Miriam does not, however, give a first-person account of her own impressions; Miss Richardson is clearly present as the narrator, relying almost entirely on third-person depiction of the novel's events. This relationship of author to narrative is not itself unusual, but the faithfulness with which Miss Richardson sustains it is, for she completely foregoes the privilege of reaching beyond Miriam's grasp of a situation to another consciousness which may perceive the event more tellingly than Miriam's. Her one point of view must suffice for both compositional focus and vehicle of attitudes and judgments. The result is a complete identification of author and heroine remarkably consistent in so long a novel.

The lesson of James was learned with advantage. The single point of view is a precise focus shaping the formal outline and the evaluative perspective of the narrative. As an element of structure, point-of-view control is primarily spatial, identifying as it does an area of awareness in both objective and subjective time. It achieves a unity—and a specification—of objective place for *Pilgrimage* and thus solidifies the objective control evident in its external time structure. The space element in a chronicle structure, we recall, becomes an aspect of time under the necessity to change, and hence we expect the *locus* of the point of view to show its own kind of change in time. In the course of so long a pilgrimage it is inevitable that Miriam—who is her consciousness—should change, developing different awarenesses. We are satisfied that the kinds of change she experiences are consonant with the time taken to represent them. But these changes are apparent to the reader in the contents of consciousness; the consciousness itself, the *locus* of impressions, is constant. Hence, as method, the single point of view accomplishes a structural balance of objective and subjective space dimensions similar to that of the two levels of time. As the constant narrative focus, simply continued from volume to volume, it stabilizes the narrative in objective space even while, as the amorphous mesh of impressions, it allows Miss Richardson the subjective freedom of its contents.

The disadvantage of the single point of view in so long a novel is the inevitable danger of monotony. To confine the reader to a single view for so long requires the novelist to create a character whose sensibility is capable of extensive and varied interest to the reader. There are limitations in this respect for Miss Richardson's heroine, who is, by design, a woman extraordinarily sensitive to her profound femininity and hence of rather specialized interest—or uninterest—from time to time in the novel. Miss Richardson surely did not regard this as a problem, but she did provide technically for relief from the third-person approach to Miriam. There are frequent shifts to a first-person rendition which allow Miriam to "speak for herself." The shift in interest is from indirect to direct presentation, usually a gain in immediacy. The integrity of the entire illusion as a single point of view is in no way destroyed, but the reader is given a varied access to that point of view in the alternation of first- and third-person presentation. The effectiveness of the shift is due as much to the stylistic contrast between the two means of presentation as to the structural variety achieved, but we shall say more about that contrast in the next chapter. It is enough here to point out the significance of the shift as structural variety possible within the single point of view.

Thematic outline, objective time limitation, and objective space limitation through a single point of view together provide the structural framework of *Pilgrimage*. It is a strict framework, and yet it is loose. It is most impressive when the twelve-volume sequence is before us. When one of the separate volumes is considered independently, it is apparent that the elements of this broad structure are operative in the organization of the individual books, but these elements are obscured there by the greater force of structural methods dependent on a different, subjective dimension of time and space.

The effect is deliberate, for Miss Richardson sought to create an essentially mimetic novel. For her, as we have observed, this meant a representation of life or existence as it is felt in the individual consciousness. The particulars of the narration, then, must be interior events, and therefore in the separate chapters we are shifted to the subjective, psychological plane of structure. Events as they occur in consciousness exhibit a fluidity of movement that is essentially irregular, both qualitatively and quantitatively nonuniform. Their structure is not the consecutive, predictable, cause-effect series of objective time, but the dynamic interpenetration of perception and memory and anticipation through significant associations.[11] Outer and inner time are not clearly disjunct, of course, and though their nature and relationships are a subject of complex inquiry, their functional relationships in human experience may be analyzed as a basis of structure in the novel without theorizing about the abstract validity of their separate existence and qualities. The balance between outer and inner achieved for the broad structure of *Pilgrimage* underlies Miss Richardson's method of composing the separate volumes where, functionally, description of the outer makes possible the revelation of the inner, felt life. The first chapter of Pilgrimage, *Pointed Roofs,* illustrates typically her method of specific structure and some of the technical devices used to effect it.

2

Pointed Roofs itself is divided into chapters, and within the chapters are sections set off by space in the print. The first chapter begins:

Miriam left the gaslit hall and went upstairs. The March twilight lay upon the landings, but the staircase was almost dark. The top landing was quite dark and silent. There was no one about. It would be quiet in her room. She could sit by the fire and be quiet and think things over until Eve and Harriett came back with the parcels. She would have time to think about the journey and decide what she was going to say to the Fräulein. (I, 15)

We are in the narrative present, observing Miriam as the narrator first introduces her. Precisely where she is, beyond the hall, the staircase, and room vaguely indicated, we do not know. Nor do we know the identity of Eve, Harriett, or the Fräulein. The narrator does not tell us; we are aware only—again without being told directly—that Miriam moves up the stairs, along the landing toward her room.

The information in the paragraph apparently is the summary of what concerns Miriam at this moment: the incidental awareness of the hall's appearance, the prospect of her quiet room, the chance to think about "the journey." The next several paragraphs are similar, describing Miriam's further movements and thoughts once she has reached her room. At her window she looks out on—and hears—"the Thursday afternoon piano-organ." She is preoccupied with some worry, merely called "it," which draws her immediate attention from the music. But then quite abruptly and standing alone as a paragraph, this sentence appears: "The organ was playing *The Wearin' o' the Green*." (I, 15) The narration then focuses just as abruptly on the "last term at school, in the summer" when Miriam first heard the tune on the organ. A brief description of remembered experiences follows:

. . . all the class shouting "Gather roses while ye may," hot afternoons in the shady north room, the sound of turning pages, the hum of the garden beyond the sun-blinds, meetings in the sixth-form study. . . . Lilla, with her black hair and the specks of bright amber in the brown of her eyes, talking about free-will. (I, 16)

The next paragraph describes Miriam stirring the fire in her room; it is followed by one giving more details of the "last summer" in school, this time modified by Miriam's regret that those days will be no more. A particular memory persists: the appearance at the tennis club on Saturday of a "white twinkling figure," the mention of whom presumably orients the next paragraph:

Why had he come to tea every Sunday—never missing a single Sunday—all the winter? Why did he say: "Play *Abide with me,"* "Play *Abide with me,"* yesterday, if he didn't care? What was the good of being so quiet and saying nothing? Why didn't he say: "Don't go," or: "When are you coming back?"? Eve said he looked perfectly miserable. (I, 16)

Within four paragraphs the reader has had to bring to focus a presumed present when Miriam stirs the fire, and an obvious past when "last summer" is described in terms of a quick catalogue of memorable sights and sounds. And within that past an unnamed figure—a man—is specified, only to be particularized further in an action which occurred in the winter just passed (it is March, we remember), an action the significance of which—to Miriam—is extended to the next sentence which describes a further action of "his" yesterday—from the point in time of the presumed narrative present. From the very beginning of the chapter to this point there are three simple occurrences in the present of the narrative, occurrences apparently insignificant in themselves and vaguely connected by their succession in time and the fact of Miriam's being there in the room doing something. Chiefly thinking; in those thoughts the narrative follows a loop through points of time in the past which are nonconsecutive but contiguous in association.

This section of the first chapter in *Pointed Roofs* ends in one further paragraph where Miriam, in the present, worries again over the prospects of her immediate future "governessing." The thought recalls something a Miss Giles had said in the past about happiness. An image of Miss Giles occurs as an afterthought: Miss Giles with "cameo brooch—long, white, flat fingered hands and that quiet little laugh." She is suddenly brought back to the present by hearing the last tune on the piano-organ; the opening of her door to admit an as yet unseen visitor breaks the reverie and ends the section.

The forward movement of the narrative in its own present is simple, unobtrusive; its continuity is achieved by a few indications of Miriam's location and activity. Forming as they do the present of the sequence, they locate the reader objectively and are the points of departure for the loops of interior time compassed in Miriam's reveries. The measure of passing time is the piano-organ which plays out its roll of tunes in a rather short time. When Miriam first hears it, the first reverie begins. She is finally brought back fully to the present when she notices that the last tune is over. Within this interval, there would be possible a much greater extent of movement backward in memory and forward in expectation than the text records. Perhaps the selection of the few such movements here can be rationalized by determining what this section accomplishes in the development of a narrative.

It is fairly certain from the outset that the reader's access to the narrative will be confined to the point of view of a single character. How else to regard the assumed identity of Eve and Harriett, the use of "it" to acknowledge what is worrying Miriam, "he" for the "white twinkling figure," and the other nebulous references throughout the section? They are given precisely as they would occur to Miriam. What she thinks and sees and feels, then, will be the extent of the reader's view of the narrative events and, more important, of his view into her character. Lacking an author's exposition of the contents of Miriam's reverie, the reader thus far in *Pointed Roofs* can comprehend only the accompanying attitudes Miriam seems to have toward her own experiences. She is troubled about an uncertain future; more, she is uncomfortably perplexed by the elusive meaning of certain past experiences. She is young enough to have been in school recently—and she was apparently happy there. Now a disruption of some kind propels her toward a frightening future. We need not puzzle long over this short section: it is initial in the novel and captures at best a fuzzy glimpse of young, tense, uncertain Miriam.

In its mode of presentation it begins subtly the work of expository introduction which the conventional omniscient author might have accomplished more explicitly—and flatly —in the same space. The structural limits of the passage are unobtrusively fixed in the brief, restricted, objective detail of time and place; the continuity is assured in the single consciousness focused. We are not given a specific "issue," germinally thematic, so much as what seems to be a random selection of momentary reflections, but is in fact a selection of expressive attitudes identifying the quality of the perceiving consciousness and specifying some of its history in experience. The attitudes link the otherwise disjunct items of memory and perception. So softened are the outlines of objective time and place, and so vague must the factual content of Miriam's reflections be at this point, that the reader is really forced to fix upon the refracting consciousness itself for "significance." This is the precise effect Miss Richardson desired to achieve; it is the basis of her method in the entire novel, however elaborated and varied that method becomes in succeeding portions of the book.

The first chapter of *Pointed Roofs* contains two other

sections, both similar to the one just examined. In the
second, Harriett has joined Miriam in her room (it was she
who opened the door at the end of the first section); the
narrative is almost entirely the dialogue between them.
We learn more about Miriam's past and future plans: The
interior time orbit—moving between past and future—
compassed in the first section as reverie, is here compassed
in the narrative present as conversation with explicit references and allusions in a logical rather than associative
connection. The third section continues the close alignment
of "moments" in objective time. It is the next morning:
first in bed, then dressing before a mirror (the device obviously gives Miss Richardson a chance to have Miriam comment on her physical make-up), talking with sister Eve,
and finally going down to breakfast. Miriam again thinks
and remembers, remembers and anticipates. By now we
know where her journey will take her and why, much about
her past, her family and friends, but chiefly her attitudes
toward all these.

The division of Chapter I into sections indicates a time
lapse (brief, in this instance) between their events, or a
modification of scene, either in place (as the third section
has Miriam in bed and in front of her mirror) or with a
different focus of attention (in the second Harriett and
Eve are added to the scene; dialogue rather than reverie is
presented). For a more radical change in time and place,
Miss Richardson begins a new chapter. Thus Chapter II of
Pointed Roofs is concerned with Miriam's journey to the
continent accompanied by her father. The sections of this
chapter are similar in pattern to those in Chapter I: a
cluster of "moments" which focus on an exterior location

or occurrence—the boat, the countryside from the window of a train, an overheard conversation—and the loops of interior past and future coiling around the external present. There is no rigidly marked point of change from exterior to interior focus, nor an inflexible period of duration for either. No action develops; time just moves, almost imperceptibly, as we are shown here and there Miriam in relation to places and people seen or remembered; speaking, meditating; her psychological character little by little revealed.

Though they seem so, the moments comprising sections and chapters are not entirely arbitrary in their selection and organization. They obviously are intended to define the quality of Miriam's responses, but the demands of change and development implicit in the time movement require accommodation in the structure. In the second part of this study we indicated the kind and extent of development Miriam achieves in *Pilgrimage* and marked out the recurrent motifs which represent—in evolving attitudes and beliefs—the areas of change: Miriam's attitude toward men; her peculiar susceptibility to ecstatic feelings, her dilemma about religion, and so on.

The contents of any section or chapter in any of the twelve volumes are by no means limited entirely to these motifs; Miss Richardson is always alert to her belief that this novel must give the impression of life fully perceived. Too obvious a pointing up of motifs would, for her, perhaps be "essayistic," and hence they are integrated in sequences of responses including trivia not immediately relevant to a motif. But the motifs are there in every book; indeed they are introduced singly in *Pointed Roofs* and thus become from the beginning a major basis of selection and structural unity in the entire novel, shaping the narrative formally and thematically. In the long third chapter of *Pointed Roofs,* for example, we are shown Miriam reacting to a number of things related to the life at Fräulein Pfaff's school. Her impressions of the girls, of the "German" atmosphere of Hanover, of the interiors of rooms—these and others are responses significantly expressive in themselves, but they sometimes provoke speculations, estimations beyond themselves, and an attitude or belief, central to what continues in later volumes as a motif, emerges. Thus a cluster of sections in the third chapter portrays Miriam during a *Vorspielen.* Each of four sections is concerned with Miriam's impressions of a performer and the piece of music played or sung. Emma Bergmann plays Chopin's fifteenth nocturne and the effect on Miriam is her first full (and, to her, frightening) "illumination" in the novel: the music lifts her into an aura of bright light which "transports" her beyond her finite surroundings. In the next section Clara Bergmann plays and the "light" comes again, this time bringing memories of a Devonshire childhood when a scene was lighted for her as is the *saal* at Fräulein's by the Bergmanns' playing. Her susceptibility to this kind of heightened feeling and its power to arouse a sense of the continuous self is the germ of a major motif.

By contrast, the next section concerns the English Martin sisters, whose playing "brought back the familiar feeling of English self-consciousness." (I, 44) They play *adagio* and *vivace* movements from a Beethoven sonata, but there is the feeling that they are straining to play the German way, "with expression" as the Bergmanns had done. Their playing is self-conscious enough to draw attention to itself, not to the "feeling" of the music. The motif has expanded to include the idea of the "joy," symbolized by light, arising out of the spontaneous, the "inner," not the self-conscious and deliberate. Thematically, this is the core motif of the novel; here it is couched in the context of Miriam's wider impressions of a superior sense of beauty among the Germans. The particular significance of the power of abstractive music to stimulate an "illumination" is blended with other evidences of Hanover's "special charm," as it would have to be in Miriam's consciousness at the moment of its impress, but it recurs later as continuing motif.

This general pattern in the first chapter is relatively stable in the other eleven chapters of *Pointed Roofs*. When we consider the volume as a unit, we are aware that some months pass (the change in seasons is made obvious in Miriam's occasional thoughts about the landscape's varying aspect) and that the illusion of all the varied experiences of crowded days is achieved in the presentation of a cluster of moments whose inner and outer concerns are representatively dense. Experiences during the sequences of interior time are organized to reflect Miriam's present interests and moods, or to signify what, as motif, will become thematically significant in succeeding moments or later volumes. It is a self-contained book bounded by what we may call the "Hanover experience," its beginning and ending simply the temporal limits of Miriam's sojourn there. It promises no episodic beginnings and endings, familiar in the consecutive actions of a plot novel; it simply moves Miriam through a series of significant experiences during a definitely fixed time and place, showing her for what she is by the quality of her responses. Its interest is therefore final even while it has equally important connections with successive volumes when the novel as a whole is considered.

Each of *Pilgrimage*'s twelve parts was published separately; years sometimes intervened between one and the next. Miss Richardson's own insistence that any volume, or part of it, can be read independently of the rest is accounted for in the organization of *Pointed Roofs*. The same would be true of any of the other volumes, developing as they do on the general principle described in *Pointed Roofs*. But ultimately the twelve volumes must be considered as a single structure.

3

Present events, as experience, become a part of the structure of memory, and hence may recur in future. When they do, they become elements of compositional structure in a stream-of-consciousness novel. The reader is reminded —by an image, a phrase, an allusion—of a prior event which, emerging in consciousness as memory, permits the reader to juxtapose its original context with that of its recollection. The otherwise separate contexts achieve thereby the connection of past and present. It is a fundamental process of consciousness and hence a fundamental element in the structure of *Pilgrimage*. To illustrate its method there, we may refer again to the thematic motif established in the *Vorspielen* sections of *Pointed Roofs,* where a certain quality of music symbolized an ideal feeling. In *Honeycomb,* when Miriam plays and sings one evening for the Corries' guests, her growing impatience with English upper middle-class "society" is partly defined to her—and the reader—in terms of "German" music, by which she means something akin to the *Pointed Roofs* insight:

"Ich grolle nicht, und wenn das Herz auch bricht," sang Miriam, and thought of Germany. Her listeners did not trouble her. . . . No English person would quite understand —the need, that the Germans understood so well—the need to admit the beauty of things . . . the need of the strange expression of music, making the beautiful things more beautiful. (I, 374)

The reference is to the way Miriam believed Emma Bergmann felt the Chopin nocturne in *Pointed Roofs.* Again, in *The Tunnel* Miriam is trying desperately to understand the world of the Wilsons when she first visits them. Attracted and repelled by it, she finds a partial answer in listening to Alma play Chopin. The Wilsons' "cultivated" life was symbolized in Alma's Chopin:

It was clear that [Alma's] taste had become cultivated, that she *knew* now, that the scales had fallen from her eyes as they had fallen from Miriam's eyes in Germany; but the result . . .
  Chopin she had never met, never felt or glimpsed. (II, 125)

Like the English Martins playing Beethoven at Hanover: "They knew, but they did not dare."
  This particular memory does not continue through the twelve volumes, nor should it; others as palpable in later

experience function similarly between later volumes. The device is used extensively to identify the intermittent well-ings-up of the stable consciousness in Miriam. Instead of the reflexive phrase or allusion, there is a recurrent image of light or a garden. The effect is the same, however, in signaling the relationship of the parts. More frequent, if less obvious, is the phrasal or allusive device. Volumes so widely separated as *The Tunnel* (the fourth) and *Dawn's Left Hand* (the tenth) are brought together thematically by this device.

Chapter VII of *The Tunnel* is about a quarter of a page long, a single paragraph which is expressive of Miriam's general dejected frame of mind in that part of the novel. She is in a London street and sees a sign, "Teetgen's Teas," which always makes her think of "her"—presumably her mother who had committed suicide recently. We know that this tragedy was the greatest personal pain she had ever experienced, and that it intensified and symbolized her feelings about the general despair and hopelessness of her life up to that moment. The short paragraph is a summary depiction of that frame of mind through a specific identification with the shop sign. Six volumes later, Miriam is in precisely the same locale and sees the shop sign:

Teetgen's Teas, she noted, in grimed, gilt lettering above a dark and dingy little shop. . . .
And *this* street, still foul and dust-filled, but full now also of the light flooding through the larger streets with which in her mind it was clearly linked, was the place where in the early years she would suddenly find herself lost and help-lessly aware of what was waiting for her eyes the moment before it appeared: the grimed gilt lettering that *forced me*

*to gaze into the darkest moment of my life and to remember
that I had forfeited my share in humanity for ever and must
go quietly and alone until the end.*

*And now their power has gone. They can bring back only
the memory of a darkness and horror, to which, then, something has happened, begun to happen?* (IV, 155-56. Miss
Richardson's italics.)

The Oberland experience has awakened Miriam; the re-
duplication of this scene confirms the change in her by
showing the reader Miriam's explicit awareness of it. And
the structural integrity of the novel is enhanced.

This method of connecting parts of the novel can be
explored further—in the use of symbolic objects, for
example, which are introduced and reintroduced strategically. The bars of the fireplace grates at home, at Banbury
Park, and at Newlands symbolize to Miriam the imprison-
ment she feels before the first cycle of freedom in her
pilgrimage. When her attention is drawn to them in
Pointed Roofs, Backwater, and *Honeycomb,* she is reminded of her plight—and so is the reader, who also sees
thereby a thematic connection between these chapters.
Similarly, the letter whose contents Miriam knows before
she opens it becomes a symbol of her new certainty of
extra-sensory perception in *Dawn's Left Hand* and is the
object which later, in *Clear Horizon,* helps the reader to
understand the core of disagreement between Miriam and
Hypo at the break-up of their affair.

4

The "perfectly rigid framework" of which Edwin Muir
spoke in describing the chronicle novel permits within its
extensive time and space limits an "arbitrary and careless

progression." The structural pattern of *Pointed Roofs,*
like that of all the individual volumes, is an adaptation of
the over-all principle of *Pilgrimage* to the specific area
of concern in a single chapter: the compositional strategy
of two levels of time and place brought together as they
are felt in a single consciousness and selected to give the
illusion of completeness as well as to define the significant
attitudes by which to gauge the development of that consciousness.

The arbitrary progression evident in the shifting and
balancing of outer and inner time, memory and perception is the "life" quality in *Pilgrimage* as a chronicle.
Its aesthetic significance to Miss Richardson is primarily
its imitative realism. But the long continuance of this
narrative so closely bound in point of view and momentary
objective time inevitably engenders monotony; its close
attention to details eventually slows down the narrative
flow to tedium. The further effects of conscious variety,
contrast, and quantitative economy are needed to enhance
the aesthetic shape of the novel. And yet these effects
cannot be achieved at the expense of imitative integrity.
Miss Richardson was doubtless aware of this and attempted to effect a solution by varying the emphasis on
inner and outer attention in Miriam's consciousness, by
adapting the contrast of scenic and pictorial presentation
to the limitations of stream of consciousness, and by use of
synopsis and syncopation within the stream.

We noted in the first chapter of *Pointed Roofs* that the
external occurrences—whether a simple identification of
time and place or an action—in the narrative present were
vague and only functionally significant, stimulating the

introspective direction of Miriam's consciousness. In the *Vorspielen* sections of the third chapter, the external events sustain Miriam's attention on themselves, drawing her consciousness to something specially meaningful in them. In both instances the emphasis is on the psychological event of her response, but a significant differentiation in method is illustrated. It was impossible for Miss Richardson to limit her narration to Miriam's past recollected through incidental reminders in an unimportant present, for the essential orientation of *Pilgrimage* is Miss Richardson's survey of a back-dated (from her point of view as narrator outside the novel), progressive present in which the past is contained as memory. Proust's method in *A la recherche du temps perdu,* by contrast, established the narrator and his present within the novel, surveying and reconstructing the past and ultimately ending in the same, extended present.

In *Pilgrimage* events in the narrative present not only revive significant memories, but themselves become memory, significant when they are rearoused by subsequent perceptions in a cumulative progression in objective time. The occurrences that sustain Miriam's attention on themselves are usually those which inform, or are informed by, a mood, a frame of mind, a particular interest or thought significant thematically or descriptively. Thus, the seemingly insignificant phenomenon of a "charming" girl's behavior at a party holds Miriam's attention for what seems a disproportionately long time in *The Tunnel.* (II, 174-76) But her observations extend the motif of man-woman relationships, informing the phenomenon itself with her current perspective and being herself informed, insofar as a new insight is added to her continual probing of that relationship.

Almost the entire ninth volume, *Oberland,* focuses Miriam's attention outward to the Swiss Alps and the experiences she shares there with other vacationers. The whole Oberland adventure achieves Miriam's mystical awakening; it profoundly informs her and hence is able to sustain her most alert attention. And as a practical device for exhibiting in Miriam what she cannot, as the excluded author, describe, Miss Richardson allows Miriam to concentrate on a scene in her physical surroundings; the impressions of it reflect the quality of Miriam's sensitiveness, itself thematically important but not always easily disengaged, for its own interest, from her concern with charming girls or socialism or bad advertisements for Dare's soap. Chapter VI of *Honeycomb,* for example, contains a group of sections which are simply Miriam's impressions of a West End street. The street is negligible —it is not even named—but her attention is fixed on it and her impressions define her own perceptiveness. Thus:

The West End street . . . grey buildings rising on either side, angles sharp against the sky . . . softened angles of buildings against other buildings . . . high moulded angles soft as crumb, with deep undershadows . . . creepers fraying from balconies . . . strips of window blossoms across the buildings, scarlet, yellow, high up; a confusion of lavender and white pouching out along the dipping sill . . . a wash of green creeper up a white painted house-front . . . patches of shadow and bright light. . . . Sounds of visible near things streaked and scored with broken light as they moved, led off into untraced distant sounds . . . chiming together. (I, 416)

These several focuses give the reader access to Miriam as a character in several perspectives. He shares the intimacy of her introspective musings, and he observes her in outer involvements—whether of passive receptivity to a scene or of thought, action, conversation with others. Miriam's complexity as a character is enhanced, but equally important is the variety of arrangement these alternations permit in a long narrative. There is no rigid pattern requiring first an inner section, then an outer, then a purely descriptive outer, and so on; that kind of contrivance would have been more deadly than the flat consistency of one focus.

There are further variations by reduplicating focuses within focuses. The first two chapters of *Revolving Lights* are a clear example of the variety possible in a spread of narrative. This seventh volume consists of only four chapters, three rather long ones and a short fourth. The entire first chapter is shaped externally by Miriam's walk home from a lecture or Lycurgan meeting. At the outset she is briefly and perfunctorily aware of the building she leaves, the dispersing crowd, the street into which she walks. Quickly her attention shifts inward to the discussion she has heard at the meeting. There follows a dense complex of thoughts about sociological speculations, her own intellectual development, the pattern of "life," all interlaced with recalled fragments of the discussion. The connections are entirely inner, associative, as her mind plays back and forth between ideas, relevant conversations with Michael and others in the past, and so on. Several pages later a brief reminder of the objective location is set out in a single sentence showing Miriam's momentary awareness of the

rich intensity of a street light. Then we plunge again into
the "disorder" of thoughts about Russian revolutionaries,
English socialism, the English character. She is abruptly
aware, in the midst of these thoughts, that she is in a "little
blue-lit street" in the West End. There is a prolonged fas-
cination with the character of the street and its houses with
pillared porticoes. This interruption illuminates the physical scene, but more importantly provides a kind of descriptive commentary on the sensibility in whose responses to
ideas we are closely involved. The street reminds Miriam
of its inhabitants and again we are eased into her inner
reflections, this time about "West End life": speculations,
judgments, memories flow diversely, coursing even through
thoughts on novels about West End life. Her mixed feelings about this life project her mind backward to Hanover,
the Pernes's school, Newlands; thence to her own family
forebears, their temperaments, their legacy to the shape
of her own character. A sentence shows us she is briefly
aware of being in Oxford Street, about which there are a
few reflections, and then it is the quality of her ancestors'
temperaments again. After a few relevant considerations
of her own developing tastes and temperament, quite suddenly there is a conversation going on between her and
another person whose identity is not definite for a page
or two more—nor is the subject of their dialogue clearly
related to her musings about her forebears or herself. In
time we learn that she is talking to Hypo Wilson, a remembered conversation during a visit in the past. The focus has
shifted again to entirely scenic (in Lubbock's sense) presentation involving Miriam in an outer concern rendered
dramatically within an intensely inner focus. During the

conversation we are returned to the present of the narrative by Miriam's occasional comments on the dialogue as she walks, but then there is the conversation again, scenically set out in its own present. The chapter continues this way to the end where Miriam has gotten to a coffee house and sits thinking until it closes. Miss Richardson has distributed the narration of inner events among the several kinds of focus, relieving both the difficulty and the monotony that a consistent, uniform stream may have created.

The procedure is exactly reversed in the second chapter of *Revolving Lights*. Its time relationship to the first is unspecified, but Miriam goes with Michael to the East End to call on some Russian revolutionaries, friends of his. Miriam's current enthusiasm for socialist theory motivates an eager curiosity to meet and talk with the Lintoffs. We might expect a predominantly outer focus, therefore, and this chapter accordingly develops much as a conventional narrative would. Continuity depends on the successive events in objective time which comprise the long visit. In the Lintoffs' hotel room Miriam is almost entirely absorbed in the conversations which Miss Richardson renders directly. The narrative bridges of commentary and reflection are Miriam's, of course, and here brief inward focuses occur as she ponders a particular remark or gesture or associative connection arising in her own mind. But the demands of the outward events soon recall her attention and the narration continues through further conversations and movements: separation of Michael and Lintoff from Miriam and Mme. Lintoff whence a new conversational line develops, movement of the four between hotel and café, observations on interesting things heard and seen, and so on. The reader is not restricted to the close confines of Miriam's thoughts; he observes her in the revealing postures of social relations, even as he is made aware of them through her point of view. The purposes of the novel in character portrayal and thematic development are served, but the emphatic use of exterior method again readjusts the reader's view to an alternative perspective complementing that of the previous chapter, without violence to the structural framework that shapes both.

The use of alternative focuses is a strategy evident in the sectional units of a chapter, as we saw in *Pointed Roofs;* in the larger chapter divisions within a volume, as we saw in *Revolving Lights;* and, though less frequently than in these former, between some volumes and their sequels. The brooding, somber *The Trap* concentrates predominantly on the inward self-searching Miriam undergoes, but *Oberland,* which follows, generally shows Miriam ecstatically out-turned to the Alpine adventure. The inner-outer distinction seems to embrace Percy Lubbock's differentiation of scenic and pictorial presentation; scenic when the event is enacted, as it were, before the reader's view, pictorial when there is "the reflection of events in the mind of somebody's receptive consciousness."[12]

The third-person narrative perspective allows Miss Richardson to use both scene and picture without lapsing from the restricted point of view. In a novel so panoramic as *Pilgrimage* we might expect a greater dependence on picture than scene, and this is in fact the case with the novel. And we might expect the use of scene when a heightened effect, an urgent immediacy is desired for critical events in the narrative. This, too, is true within the framework of the inner-outer focuses, but often both scene and picture occur within one or the other focus. In the first chapter of *Revolving Lights* we noted that during her reverie along the West End walk Miriam recalls an extended episode with Hypo which is rendered scenically, as though it were happening then in the reader's view. In its context the event achieves importance by being rendered thus, an importance only partly attributable to thematic selection, however. The summarized picture of her ancestors has equal significance to Miriam's understanding of herself, but it is not accorded a scene. Miriam can *recall* a scene with Hypo, but not one with ancestors several generations back, obviously. It is not a question of relative importance, but psychological plausibility. Thus the Hypo episode is recalled as scene, and Miss Richardson is provided an opportunity to present another character directly to the reader and within Miriam's point of view; he is engaged in an action (verbal, physical, or both) with her, but disengaged from her during the intervening impressions necessary to pictorial presentation. The reader himself sees the second character in relation to Miriam—contrastively, complementarily—or observes him to say something significant about her. The shift, then, from picture to scene may be essentially a strategy for taking the reader directly to Miriam's inclusive, social dimension as a character, as well as a means to simple variety and the heightening of some events for specific thematic importance.

The contingent difficulty is a leveling of presumably uneven events; the kind of leveling that provoked Katherine Mansfield once to remark that "everything being of equal importance to [Miriam], it is impossible that everything should not be of equal unimportance."[13] For example, so critical an event in Miriam's development as her first attendance at a Quaker meeting is a pictured, summarized impression, remembered during a reverie in her room after the Lintoff visit. Presented thus, it does not itself occur in the narrative present, even though it is developed in some detail as pictured past. On the other hand, in *The Trap* Miss Richardson develops scenically an episode in which Miriam and her roommate prepare for bed in their new flat, talking all the while and eventually, hilariously (certainly for the reader) discovering bed-bugs in the bedding. The events are uneven if we assume that quantitative rather than qualitative selection should explain their initial inclusion and hierarchical relationship in *Pilgrimage*. Quantitative selection—selection "in accordance with the principle of artistic economy . . . on the grounds of the inherent interest or contribution to the plot of each incident"[14]—is inevitable in any novel; certainly it is impossible to conceive of one compassing eighteen years in twelve books without rather stringent selection of this kind. The significant selection in *Pilgrimage*, however, is qualitative—selection "on the grounds of being typical of what happens in real life, whether on the plane of external action or on the plane of internal sequences of sense-impressions, thoughts or feelings."[15] The vagaries of consciousness, creating their own order and rank, exhibit the very "unevenness" Miss Richardson intentionally represented. Moreover, she had to exhibit what, in her view, is qualitatively distinctive of the feminine consciousness: its natural capacity for absorbing with equal interest the multiple and diverse elements of experience; its "shapeless shapeliness," when not misdirected by evanescent systems and dogmas, partial principles and judgments.

The time element is crucial here. If felt life for Miriam exhibits these qualities, it must do so in the present of the things experienced, whether that present is chiefly recollection of the past or not. Controlled as it is by a single point of view and an objective time movement in the progressive present, *Pilgrimage* can convey only what Miriam knows or feels as her experiences occur. The self-realization achieved finally in *Dimple Hill* culminates a search for reality; it is the perspective which develops through the many experiences preceding it. But the *present* of those prior experiences cannot be seen from that developed perspective, even though they are ultimately contained in it. Miriam recalls the Quaker meeting, her family history, and other disjunct events in the same present of *Revolving Lights,* but she does not have there the perspective of *Dimple Hill* to see their comparative significance. At the moment Miriam experiences them as memory and reflection, however, they exhibit the way of consciousness in real life, and hence in their imbalance they are faithful to Miss Richardson's commitment to mimetic representation. Inner and outer focus, scene and picture, therefore, are to be understood generally in their "life" dimension; their "art" dimension in the novel is generally their use for contrast and variety, for broad effects in method of narration and method of arrangement. The two dimensions do not clash for Miss Richardson; one is but the organ of the other's function.

Thus, Miss Richardson forsook the conventional methods

of the novelist's art for new ones, or recast them for new uses in her aim to imitate subjective life fictionally. She was indeed liberated from the arbitrariness of conventions for which she saw no counterpart in felt life. But however free its form and broad its thematic selection, a novel is still an art form, not life itself, and therefore quantitative selection is inevitable for artistic economy. There must be a technical means, supplementary to theme, which keeps the narrative moving in time, distinguishing the important from the less important, the event of general interest from that of specific interest, and sustaining thereby the thematic focus of the book and the reader's interest in continuing it. This is true whether that movement is vertical, as when consciousness is explored in depth, or horizontal in occurrences on the objective plane. Miss Richardson has preserved little of the conventional means to this economy. The ordinary mechanics of suspense, for example, are useless; there is no plot in which to arrange conflicts, climaxes, resolutions. Even the alternations of picture and scene do not always assure it. A pictured impression may be general, specific or both; a scene, directly enacting an event, may require instances of summary or foreshortening for its own effect. The technique of synoptic narration is unavoidable: it telescopes time, summarizes events, continues sequences; it achieves qualitative selection while preserving the sense of time movement fundamental to narrative.

Because so little of the eighteen-year span is presented as the narrative present in *Pilgrimage,* it is understandable that between book and book large gaps of time should sometimes exist. The reader is not really denied any pertinent incident occurring between them, because her great reliance on Miriam's recollections for matter allows Miss

Richardson to draw the relevant events of the gap into the memory structure of the moments in succeeding volumes. Nor in a cluster of moments comprising sections or chapters in books is an external indication of passing time necessary when those moments are contiguous and are identified to the reader, vaguely or explicitly as points of time in the objective present. When neither compensation serves her— when, for example, the objective present itself, not memory, is the focus of attention—Miss Richardson adapts conventional synopsis to her purposes.

In *The Trap,* the progress of the narrative at one point requires the passage of an entire season between episodes. The gap is not to be accounted for in specific memories, and the relationship between the two chapters is not clearly contiguous in time, place, or nature of experiences. Hence Miss Richardson supplies an intervening chapter which telescopes in a few lines the passing of spring and its general effect on Miriam; presented, of course, as Miriam's own impressions but without any external context of place and time for the summary.[16]

More conventionally, the same necessity accounts for synopsizing at the beginning of a chapter separated sharply in time and place from the preceding one. Thus at the beginning of Chapter III of *Deadlock:*

Three months ago, Christmas had been a goal for which she could hardly wait. It had offered her, this time, more than the usual safe deep firelit seclusion beyond which no future was visible. . . . (III, 85)

The paragraph continues summarizing the time up to the holiday, the present of Chapter III. Chapter I takes place at the end of summer, Chapter II the first cold days of

autumn. The business of Chapter III—the Christmas visit
with sisters Eve and Harriett—is initiated by synoptic
reference to a period of time including the business of
Chapters I and II. The Christmas focus is thus fitted into
the noncontinuous experiences of the first chapters and also
bridges the time gap between the second and third.

The extent to which Dorothy Richardson uses synoptic
statement within a section or chapter already initiated is
limited. It is likely to be a single brief remark or a short
paragraph indicating a break in the narrative. In the first
chapter of *Interim* Miriam visits her friends the Brooms.
Part of a conversation about childhood Christmases is
presented directly to the reader, but with this obvious cut:

> "Did you have a Noah's *ark*," she asked, smiling at the
fire.
> "Yes; Florrie had one. Uncle George gave it to her."
> They began describing.
> "Didn't you love it?" broke in Miriam presently. (II, 298)

The summary statements could as easily be Miriam's as
Miss Richardson's. Again, in *Deadlock,* Miriam and
Michael argue about her mystical feeling for spring. The
repartee is directly rendered, until Miriam answers a question which apparently concludes the significant part of the
debate. Thus:

> "I'm perfectly sure I shall always feel the spring; perhaps
more and more." She escaped into irrelevant speech, hurrying
along so that he should hear incompletely until she had firm
hold of some far-off topic; dreading the sound of his voice.
> (III, 149)

Later, in a scene otherwise dependent on dialogue, enough time elapses between one particular and its rejoinder to justify this descriptive summary of the pause:

But she turned swiftly, leading the way down a winding side path and demanding angrily as soon as they were alone how it was possible to be too individualistic. (III, 149)

The difficulty of effecting such synopses is apparent when we consider the restriction under which Miss Richardson is working as author. The synopses must in effect be Miriam's. The last two examples cited show Miss Richardson more nearly present as author than in any other narrative situation. The more typical means of telescoping the narrative—typical, that is, of the absence of the intrusive author—is perhaps better described as syncopation than as synopsis. There are omissions from the sequence of events, but no statements to summarize them. The episode continues, let us say scenically, and there appears to be no break when in fact there is a deliberate one.

During Miriam's Christmas visit with her sisters, Harriett goes to her room one morning and chides her for sleeping with the window open in very cold weather:

"I love it," said Miriam, watching Harriett's active little moving form battle with the flying draperies. "I'm revelling in it."

"Well, I won't presume to shut it; but revel *up*. Here you are. Breakfast's nearly ready. Hold the ends while I get out and shut the door."

A brief paragraph follows in which Miriam's reflections on her desire for fresh air and open windows are explicitly rendered. Then:

Gerald was pouring out coffee. In the kitchen the voices of Harriett and Mrs. Thimm were railing cheerfully together. Harriett came in with a rush, slamming the door. "Is it too warm for you in here, Miss Henderson?" she asked as she drove Gerald to his own end of the table. (III, 95)

The time involved in Miriam's reflections on fresh air does not explicitly fill the breach between Harriett's remark about shutting the door and Miriam's appearance in the dining room where she can be aware of Gerald's pouring coffee. But the reflections shift attention inward to a brief but careful movement in psychological time which gives the illusion of enough external passage of time to permit Miriam's activities between getting out of bed and seeing Gerald pour the coffee. The syncopation is clearly the narrator's, but the advantage here is the absence of a verbalized summary drawing attention to her. The strategy is capable of elaborate modifications, as the first four pages of *Clear Horizon* will show.

There is a consequent density where synopsis or syncopation occurs, and the illusion of unmediated, undifferentiated events caught as they occur is preserved. It is to that illusion we must refer these as well as the other methods of presentation which we have been discussing if we are to generalize their relevance to the total compositional structure of *Pilgrimage*.

The illusion which Miss Richardson's novel achieves cannot be described in terms of symbolic structures or mythic patterns invoked to organize the chaos that, to the artist, is life or experience. Finding within the feminine experience of that ferment itself a meaning which, to her, stabilizes it, Miss Richardson had at hand the method of her novel: to show the achievement of that meaning by recording the myriad facets of life in which it germinates. She would not *impose* a meaning or pattern to create in art a form impossible in consciously felt life. The painter's stylized bird is not really truer or better as a bird than one on the wing, she seems to say.

The province of the shaping artist was therefore shifted away from plot, form, design. *Pilgrimage* does indeed have a thematic structure and a formal composition—deliberately irregular; only broadly consistent—to support it. But the novelistic art in its separate parts has been restricted to bringing into relief the "disorder" which the art of Joyce or Mrs. Woolf, let us say, was intended to control. Selection and composition are evident in *Pilgrimage,* but paradoxically so, impressing us that there is none. Picture and scene, synopsis and synopation, inner and outer focuses are techniques for arranging and unfolding the narrative, but they support no regularized scheme.

For the aesthetic support she has denied herself by shunning symbolic or analogous patterns in myth or music, she depends on the aesthetic values of complexity, immediacy, variety and contrast as they may inhere in a representation of felt life. For example, *Pilgrimage* exhibits in its entire sequence of chapters a broad contrasting alternation of moods that is a rhythmic movement of the novel; we would have to say specifically the rhythm of alternating qualities of feeling implicit in the mystic's quest. The general joyousness of *Pointed Roofs* is succeeded by the general gloom of *Backwater. Honeycomb* returns the arc to happiness; in its very last pages the mood is brought low again. Thence the

arc rises again through *The Tunnel* and *Interim* to the uncertain tension of *Revolving Lights.* It falls again to dejection and gloom in *The Trap. Oberland* swings to an almost
ecstatic happiness which is waveringly threatened in the
smaller alternations of Miriam's "purgation" in *Dawn's
Left Hand. Clear Horizon* is the final uncertainty before
the full joy of Miriam's satisfied quest in *Dimple Hill.*

Similarly, the specific devices of narrative art are adapted
to create the illusion of the activity of feminine consciousness; their aesthetic effect consists largely in their adequacy
for representing the complexity and variety of that activity.
Dense, full, various, *Pilgrimage* surmounts the difficulty
Miss Richardson found in her first efforts to represent
reality in conventional narrative: "the revelation, whence-
soever focused, of a hundred faces, any one of which, the
moment it was entrapped within the close mesh of direct
statement, summoned its fellows to disqualify it."[17] The
"rich fabric of life" cannot be stated; it can be only contemplated. Then *suggestion,* if not statement? Include all the
"fellows," or create the illusion that none has been excluded, and let them be contemplated, rousing the reader's
"contemplative consciousness"? An indirect signification of
real life by presenting the direct experience of it? The
idiom of poetry?

Such seem Miss Richardson's requisites for the novel
become poem, the novel embracing the "rich fabric of
life." The reader finds himself, she says,

. . . within a medium whose close texture, like that of poetry,
is everywhere significant and although, when the tapestry
hangs complete before his eyes, each portion is seen to enhance the rest and the shape and intention of the whole grows

clear, any single strip may be divorced from its fellows without losing everything of its power and of its meaning.

She is reviewing *Finnegans Wake*. What she says further about reading Joyce's book applies equally to her own— and it defines the theoretical basis for her neglect of conventional methods of structure:

Let us take the author at his word. Really release consciousness from literary preoccupations and prejudices, from the self-imposed task of searching for superficial sequences in stretches of statement regarded horizontally, or of setting these upright and regarding them pictorially, and plunge, provisionally, here and there; enter the text and look innocently about. . . . The coalescence and the somebody can wait.[18]

CHAPTER IV

Elaborating the Ornate Alias

THE TEXTURE of the medium in which one finds one-self when reading a stream-of-consciousness novel, Miss Richardson contends, is, like that of poetry, everywhere significant. We might omit a comma and thus amend her statement to read "is like that of poetry," and add further that the chief functional significance of that medium is the revelation of the texture or quality of the consciousness explored. This being true, when the quality of a particular sensibility is the emphatic concern of the novelist of the subjective, two difficulties for his narrative present themselves. The concentration on psychic behavior sacrifices the possibility of an adequate objectification of that sensibility in concrete actions. And the nature of mental activity itself, if represented realistically, demands flexibilities and functions of language beyond its conventional structures and usages for discursive or descriptive communication. Both difficulties are a part of what Mr. Robert Humphrey calls the problem of privacy: the problem of representing private values, associations, and relationships peculiar to a specific consciousness and yet meaningful to the reader.[1] Mr. Humphrey and some other recent students of the stream-of-consciousness novel have analyzed the various techniques effected to solve the problem.[2] But giving the greater attention to Joyce, Mrs. Woolf, and sometimes Faulkner, they have indicated general characteristics of Dorothy Richardson's "impressionistic" style without adequately specifying its nature or its function in the organic whole of *Pilgrimage*.

They have defined three devices which correspond stylistically with the three areas of consciousness to which these novelists give the reader access: sensory impression to render "pure" sensation when the thinking mind is passive; interior monologue to render discontinuous fragments of thought and impression unformulated at a speech level; and internal analysis to render the summary or analysis of deliberate speech-level thought formulations.[3] In all of them the author's problem is to make the language of these devices meaningful as representation and presentation. We are reminded that "the writer attempting to create the illusion of a mind flowing with thought and image and impression turns to the symbolist poet; he calls upon all the devices of prosody, exploiting the resources of the language in the belief that it is the writer's task to make the word fit the thought, to match the language of the mind and if necessary to invent a language that will render it."[4] To accomplish this task, Miss Richardson developed a characteristic mode of expression; it will be valuable to see how her style makes use of the resources of language to depict her chosen area and content of consciousness, and its capacity to reflect the thematic intent of the novel.

I

Without plot, the immediacy of objective, concrete action is sacrificed in *Pilgrimage*. The author withdraws herself

to a minimal function of objective narrator. We are left
with Miriam's thoughts and impressions, whose succession
and change constitute the essential evidence of time movement in narrative. Theirs is also the burden of objectifying
feeling and mood, of assuming an expressive character
functionally equivalent to action—this without an author
who explains, supplements, annotates Miriam's consciousness. Imagery—particularizing; objectifying; suggesting
rather than stating; unifying a complex of perception and
associative ideas and feelings in communicative form—is
Dorothy Richardson's chief stylistic device for making
Miriam's stream of thought and sensation privately significant and publicly meaningful. We will regard the image as
a representation, chiefly pictorial, of sensational experience,
either merely descriptive or a complex of sensation, emotion, and thought.

The description of objects, persons, or places which
importantly or incidentally catch Miriam's attention is the
first impressive use of image the reader notices in *Pilgrimage*. Early in the novel one encounters descriptions of seemingly insignificant things like this brief awareness during a
walk through a German countryside:

Standing and moving in the soft air was the strong sour
smell of baking Schwarzbrot. A big bony-browed woman
came from a dark cottage and stood motionless in the low
doorway, watching them with kindly body. (I, 114-15)

The brief, economical movement from one image to the
other suggests the fleeting impressions they are. And yet
they are neither vague nor cliché. The central content of the
image identifying the smell of baking bread is sensuous,

precise: "strong sour smell." But the image's effectiveness in conveying Miriam's particular awareness of the smell is unusually achieved by adding to the olfactory detail "standing and moving in the soft air," a kinetic dimension, animating the smell, setting it in visible motion. The image of the woman has a precise center in the visual detail of "big bony-browed," identifying rather clearly her physical mass and rough-hewn countenance. But then comes "watching them with kindly body," and the whole aspect of the woman, until then physical, is spiritualized. The transformation in both images proceeds from a precise, immediately recognizable detail—sensuous in both instances—and by deliberate surprise invests the thing imaged with a quality fundamentally true of the thing but in superficial disharmony with the central detail. One has to recall the transforming detail for the bread because it precedes the mention of the object (rather, the "smell") itself. And one has to adjust his mind to a "kindly" body that "watches." But one focuses intently on this striking perception of the peculiar mode of reality that the smell of baking bread and the *Frau* have for Miriam.

Generally, such images depend on sensuous details precisely described; often a single detail suffices to suggest the character of the whole. Precision without fullness underlies the effectiveness of this image in *Oberland,* where Miriam is unusually alert to the visible beauty of the Swiss Alps as the sun appears at dawn:

And in a moment she had seen for ever the ruby gleaming impossibly from the topmost peak: stillness of joy held still for breathless watching of the dark ruby, set suddenly like a signal upon the desolate high crag.

It could not last, would soon be plain sunlight.

Already it was swelling, growing brighter, clearing to crimson. In a moment it became a star with piercing rays that spread and slowly tilted over the upper snow a flood of rose. (IV, 96)

One does not have to read far in any of the twelve chapters before coming on this kind of description. Some volumes seem more densely imagistic than others, as we shall see later, but wherever such passages occur we are conscious of the reason for some critics' view that Miss Richardson's style is comparable to that of the Imagist poets: "clarity, precision, the intense subjectivity of impression allied with the objectivity of the realist."[5]

The imagery is by no means simply functional, as in the quoted examples, at a descriptive level, illuminating the varied environments which stimulate Miriam. The quality of Miriam's acute perceptiveness is represented equally with the particularity of the German woman or the Alpine scene. The environments must ultimately be referred to the sensibility which screens them for us; a sensibility not passive, of course, not merely absorbing impressions which are represented for us. Attitudes emerge; Miriam's sensitivity is overlaid with valuating feelings or ideas, themselves relicts of valuated impressions. Imagery to suggest feeling-responses over and above primary sensations, and yet not formulated as ideas, is necessary to Miss Richardson's method. Thus, a sense of "good" feeling is apparent in this impression of the dinner table at Mrs. Corrie's when Miriam first arrived at Newlands:

... the table like an island under the dome of the low-hanging rose-shaded lamp, the table-centre thickly embroidered with beetles' wings, the little dishes stuck about, sweets, curiously crusted brown almonds, sheeny grey-green olives; the misty beaded glass of the finger bowls— . . . the four various wine glasses at each right hand, one on a high thin stem, curved and fluted like a shallow tulip, filled with hock; and, floating in the warmth amongst all these things the strange, exciting, dry sweet fragrance coming from the mass of mimosa, a forest of little powdery blossoms . . . (I, 355)

There is simple enumeration of items here, without an explicit statement of approval or delight. And yet the sense of Miriam's pleasure is apparent in the attention to the sensuous richness her impressions suggest. The single word "warmth" summarizes the total impression; the particular pleasure of each item is implicit in its description.

By contrast, the image of the schoolroom in Banbury Park suggests its depressive effect on Miriam:

Miriam saw a long wide dining-room table covered with brown American cloth. Shelves neatly crowded with books lined one wall from floor to ceiling. Opposite them at the far end of the room was a heavy grey marble mantelpiece, on which stood a heavy green marble clock frame. At its centre a gold-faced clock ticked softly. Opposite the windows were two shallow alcoves. In one stood a shrouded blackboard or an easel. (I, 191)

Specific words ("brown," "grey," "heavy," "shrouded") assure the expression of mood or feeling about the room. The descriptive adjective achieves the communication by suggestion; no statement is necessary.

The mood in both examples is Miriam's, stimulated by or carried to the objects of her attention. When such a feeling or mood is sustained for any length of time, the images which suggest it assume a subtle relationship and, by extension, this ties one part of the narrative to another. The predominant joyousness of *Pointed Roofs* is succeeded by the dreariness of *Backwater,* and the characteristic mood is apparent in the imagery. We can illustrate the contrasting pattern in *The Trap* and *Oberland. The Trap* begins with images of decay, dissolution, impoverishment, as Miriam inspects her new residence:

She found her number to the right, just beyond the opening, on a blistered door, whose knocker, a blurred, weather-worn iron face, gazed sadly downwards. (III, 399)

She sees a dust-covered shop window nearby:

Dust lay even upon the large grey cat compactly curled amongst the sharp angles and looking forth with a green eye, glass-clear and startlingly bright in contrast to the dried socket from which its fellow should have shone. (III, 400)

The air inside the house was "dense with shut-in odours dried brown by stale pipe-smoke." (III, 400) A complexity of figures is apparent in these examples; there are single descriptive adjectives, visual images, and metaphor dependent on synesthesia. But our immediate concern is with the emotional force of Miriam's selection of details and their expressive continuity. "Dried," "blistered," "weather-worn," "dried brown," "dust" are of a piece emotionally. The significance of dejection in *The Trap* was pointed out in the second chapter of this study. The service of style in sustaining the mood which importantly organizes the many experiences of that book is apparent in the continuity of the imagery. Single images are not repeated or expanded to become symbols operative within the volume, but they are continued, connected in their capacity to concretize a single nonverbalized "feeling" which characterizes the book. We could call the feeling despair, defeat, disillusionment, frustration. To Miriam, for example, even her rooms in Flaxman Court "stood defined, mean and dismal, crushing her . . . set above a thick ascending darkness where other lives were hemmed and crushed. . . ." (III, 447) The intensity of the mood is coordinate with the violence which many of the images suggest. Her sister Harriett's bad fortune—scarcely better than Miriam's—is summarized thus:

Gerald and Harriett. Drawn, driven, washed about by tides they do not see. Flung on rocks, washed off and flung forward. (III, 503)

Miss Richardson is able to continue this tone even in Miriam's impressions of a Lycurgan party, where her growing disenchantment is felt in this image:

Wandering eyes were growing rarer, though still newcomers arrived and toured hopefully. Groups were forming of people masked, or visibly bored, sustaining the familiar. Wit, surrounded, was hard at work. (III, 488)

At its worst, Miriam's mood—and the book's tone—is objectified in images of foulness and sordidness. On a summer night, lying in her bed, Miriam registers the smells and sounds of Flaxman Court as palpable evidence of life as it seems then:

... the reek of cats comes up and in. All the summer it has come in. ...

Hoarse-voiced lovers lingering on after the roistering has died down. ...

Night long, through open windows, thick, distorted voices in strife. Shut in, maddened. Maddened confined men. Women despairingly mocking. Worst of all, children's voices sane and sweet in protest, shrilling up, driven by fear, beyond the constriction of malformed throats, into sweetness. (III, 499-500)

The integrity of the book is enhanced by this sustained centrality of mood suggested by the imagery.

We could classify this imagery as simile or metaphor or simple adjectival modification; all these forms are present, and all are to be found in the impressions of things or actions or people which impinge on Miriam's consciousness. With those images that convey an important attendant feeling, as with the more purely descriptive ones, it is the great reliance on sensuous effects—predominantly visual, auditory, kinetic, olfactory—which distinguishes simile and metaphor alike; they are consistently concrete in their representation. However, there does seem to be some correlation throughout *Pilgrimage* between the relative intensity of Miriam's stimulations and Miss Richardson's use of metaphor. It is apparent in some of the quoted passages from *The Trap;* it is even more so in *Oberland* where there is a sustained lyric ecstasy in Miriam's reactions to her Swiss holiday. We recall the crucial importance of this experience in Miriam's mystic quest, its transformation of her attitude toward past life and future. With the resources in memory, feeling, and perception focused singly for her in the unifying perspective of "awakening," it is not amiss to draw a parallel with this quality of mind and the preponderance of metaphor, which itself synthesizes, focuses the disparate or discontinuous in a single perception. By contrast, simile preserves two members of a comparison separately: "My love is like a red, red rose" presents "love" and "red rose" in existence apart, even as it invites the acceptance of their similarity. The total sensibility of the person seems singly and immediately apparent in metaphoric perception. This representation of Miriam's joy on first arriving in the Alps illustrates this effect of metaphor:

Hovering vehement above them all [the travelers insensitive to the thrill] hung the cloud of her pity for those who had never bathed in strangeness—and its dark lining, the selfish congratulation that reminded her how at the beginning of her life, in the face of obstructions, she had so bathed and now under kindly compulsion was again bathing. (IV, 24)

The pity-cloud figure gives a double signification to the image: the projection of Miriam's feeling of pity toward the "non-bathing" travelers in a striking visual suggestion of their "being beclouded"; and, by inference, her wish that the cloud which threatens them (it is "vehement") be the force of pity to initiate them to the bath in strangeness. The bath figures resume the cloud figure but with the implied difference of potential and actual immersion in the beauty of the Alps.

The rapid succession of metaphors that together compose a single picture representing Miriam's ecstatic apprehension of a varied environment is evident here:

Sungilt masses beetling variously up into pinnacles that truly
cut the sky, high up beyond their high-clambering pinewoods,
where their snow was broken by patches of tawny crag. She
still longed to glide forever onwards through that gladness
of light. (IV, 29)

Clouds that beetle, mountain peaks that cut, trees that
clamber, the vision of her own flight among them—a succession of discrete metaphors capturing the quality of each
item and composing themselves quickly into an image of
motion and vibrancy, subtly colored ("sungilt," "tawny").
Throughout *Oberland* it is as though the sustained excitement of Miriam's sensibility quickens her powers of acute
perceptiveness. The unusual frequency of color words,
particularly "gold" and "rose," is significant. There seems
to be a greater preponderance of intensive imagistic effects
like synesthesia, which extends the synthetic effect of metaphor in making Miriam's impressions precise. Emerging
into the sunlight from a low cloud through which she
rides, high on a mountain road, Miriam is aware that
"Colour was coming from above, was already here in
dark brilliance, thundery." (IV, 29) And the oxymoron
"dark brilliance" is equally effective.

    In another chapter of the novel, Miss Richardson em-
ploys an unusual mode of personification to vivify an intense conflict going on in Miriam's mind. She watches a
group of dancers, investing them with a single being which
speaks to her about her decision to quit teaching:

"You are an idiot to go on doing it. It's wrong. Lazy,"
laughed the dancers crowding and flinging all round her. "I
ought," she responded defiantly, "to stay on and make myself
into a certificated teacher." "Certificated?" they screamed,

wildly sweeping before her in strange lines of light. "If you
do you will be like Miss Cramp. Certificates—little conceited
papers, and you dead. Certificates would finish you off—Kill
—Kill—Kill—*Kill*—*Kill!*" Bang. The band stopped and
Miriam felt the bar of her chair wounding her flesh. (I, 322)

In this instance we are beyond chiefly descriptive or
attitudinally suggestive imagery. Conscious thought is
imaged by allowing Miriam's view of the dancers to
merge their movements with her thoughts. The dancers
become almost allegorical figures dramatizing the dispute
between two impulses in Miriam's own consciousness.
With this striking objectification of the contents of mind,
we become conscious of the use of imagery to extend narrative exposition beyond the requirements of the momentary impression, for here is in fact a critical condition of
mind summarizing the direction of the book's events to
that point and providing a reflexive significance to the un-
organized details preceding it. It is this very dilemma
about continuing as a teacher which is the conflict motivating the immediate change in Miriam's circumstances that
produces the next volume, *Honeycomb,* and—more re-
motely—future steps on her pilgrimage.

Functioning in the place of discursive exposition, the
image must draw together a sensation of things observed,
the complex of attitudes and judgments which attend the
impression, and, as a means of forwarding the narrative,
its reflexive relations with other parts of the narrative.
But by its nature, the image is suggestive, not explicit,
and the reader's burden is to read the image in relation to
the context of its appearance as Miriam's perception or
memory. (Though it has this function, the "certificate"

passage previously quoted is not typical of the device in
Pilgrimage because it does not allow some particular of
the exterior occurrence imaged—the dancers—to suggest
its own extended significances; Miriam transforms the
dance to something other than itself.) For example, in
Honeycomb Miriam is with her ailing mother at a resort.
Some of the other guests are kind and sympathetic to the
mother and daughter, but Miriam considers the subtle
relationship broadly:

But she knew mother was different. All of them [the other
women] knew it in some way. They spoke to her now and
again with deference, their faces flickering with beauty. They
knew she was beautiful. Sunny and sweet and good, sitting
there in her faded dress, her face shining with exhaustion.
(I, 479)

The interest of this passage as a picture of the ailing
mother conceals the strategy of reflexive reference which
composes it. The "deference" Miriam observes recalls the
fact of Mrs. Henderson's having enjoyed a comfortable
middle-class life until Mr. Henderson's recent loss of fortune. In the mother's infrequent appearances in previous
narrative, the reader has been shown the quality of her
being (sunny, sweet, good) and of her life (the serene
naïveté of middle-class refinement). She is now very ill and
despondent, yet that quality is apparent—and impressive to
the other women—even as she sits in her "faded dress," her
face "shining with exhaustion," ironic symbols of her present destitution. The history of Mrs. Henderson generalized
here is equally the history of Miriam's life as she views
it at this moment. The irony of Mrs. Henderson's crush-

ing "existence" bearing her down in spite of the "life" she owns (the women are still impressed, but by this or her vestigial gentility?—the irony is compounded) profoundly recapitulates the tension of Miriam's own distress. It also fairly summarizes the character of Miriam's total experiences through the end of *Honeycomb*. What might otherwise have to be explained or described analytically in a novel is present here in the power of the image to direct the reader's apprehension to its immediate significance and to its reflexive relationship with other parts of the context.

2

The essential problem of narrative scope for Miss Richardson, of course, is to present a succession of impressions which represent the several areas of Miriam's consciousness under the temporal necessity to change. The uses of imagery which we have discussed thus far tend to emphasize impressions from a level of consciousness between pure sensation and speech formulation; in them Miriam's mind is not passive at the level of technical sense impression, nor active in the degree that characterizes speech. When occasionally there is this passive receptivity to sense data, when Miriam does not seem to direct her impressions toward verbalized attitudes or thoughts, a pure impression is rendered, as when Miriam gazes into the windows of some Regent Street shops:

. . . bright endless caverns screened with glass . . . the bright teeth of a grand piano running along the edge of darkness, a cataract of light pouring down its raised lid; forests of hats; dresses shining against darkness, bright headless crumpling stalks; sly, silky, ominous furs; metals, cold and clanging, brandishing the light; close prickling fire of jewels . . . (I, 417)

But the greater part of *Pilgrimage* is concerned with the area of pre-speech and speech level thought. The occurrence of passages of pure sense impression is much more frequent in the early volumes; indeed, it is unusual to discover in the later volumes one comparable in purity to the shop-window occurrence. In later volumes, the area of consciousness rendered is emphatically, though not exclusively, that of directed thought at speech level; the impressions, as events, are stimuli to meditative, reflective thought about the events, not the sensation of an event for its own sake. The change is due to the maturity in intellectual perspective and emotional poise progressively achieved by Miriam in the culminating volumes. At the beginning of *Pilgrimage,* we recall, Miriam is in late adolescence; the spontaneous, exuberant quality of her reactions is typical. It is to be expected that the imagery should often be exuberantly and simply sensuous. At the same time, Miriam is not incapable of thought, of course, but even that is frequently unqualified assertiveness typical of her sense impressions. As the impressions tend in the later volumes to become more concerned with instants of connected, analytical thought, there is less need to rely on richly sensuous and suggestive imagery. It is too long to quote here, but a revealing comparison might be drawn between Miriam's reactions during a Wagner opera (IV, 171-72) and those at the *Vorspielen* in *Pointed Roofs* (I, 42-44).

This modulation in Miss Richardson's style thus serves

the fundamental necessity for time movement in narrative by imitating the effect of time on the consciousness of the central character. If it is argued that Miss Richardson's later volumes exhibit an improved literary style, this is largely true because the later Miriam is an "improvement" in sensibility over the early, sometimes cloyingly intense Miriam, and Miss Richardson was at pains to imitate both aspects faithfully.

As we have described it, this change in the use of imagery to reflect the mutations of character through time is more quantitative than qualitative. Is there a change in the content of the imagery parallel to this later, significant change in frequency? We observed earlier that the images in *Pilgrimage* may best be described together as highly sensuous, tending to the visual, auditory, kinetic, and olfactory, and as highly precise in detail. We could classify them further as favoring colors that become symbolic through recurrent use to identify moods or feelings: e.g., blue for serenity (especially the blue of the sea or sky); rose and gold for heightened joy; grey for lonely sadness. Or as drawing their comparisons (when simile or metaphor) between the world of nature and various human experiences: the sea, flowers, sunshine are prominent. Or even as tending to synesthesia. For the most part, however, the imagery in the later volumes is little different in these respects from that of the earlier ones, except perhaps in a hard-to-define difference in intensity attributable to the lower, more moderate emotional key of Miriam's growing serenity.

There is an important exception to these observations. What we have been describing is the depiction in images of Miriam's superficial consciousness, as Miss Richardson would call it. It is the empirical self of sights and sounds, ideas and thoughts—absorbing, responding here and there in its experience of the phenomenal world. But for Miss Richardson, we recall, there is a stable consciousness, a transempirical self sometimes stimulated phenomenally, sometimes independently assertive, but always indicative of the real and eternal manifesting itself. These ideas under-lie Miriam's eventual mysticism, the growth of which is signaled by Miss Richardson's use of its chief image: light. It is *the* persistent and undeviating image in *Pilgrimage* in respect to significance; perhaps, therefore, it is a variously structured symbol, standing for the transcendent real and its presence in phenomenal experience and in Miriam's feelings of heightened being. It is a central means of structural continuity from its appearance in *Pointed Roofs* to Miriam's identity of God and the light in *Dimple Hill*.

In the early chapters, the images of light usually signify simple good feeling, most intense when stimulated by music, gardens, or wide natural scenes. In time Miriam her-self comes to relate these illuminations to her earliest memory of the beauty of a sunlit garden. Thenceforth this early experience is a refuge within the self as memory accessible in contemplation. We have already traced Miriam's search for the feeling of transcendence in her existence in the "world"; when she succeeds, the images which communicate her reaction have a single pattern: light appears about and within her; it "streams" into or out of objects and people. We come to associate the image with a value, judging the experience thus illuminated as directly embodying something of the character of stable reality, its power to bring the "light" to Miriam. It is description and commentary, as when Dr. Densley surprises Miriam with a hoped-for proposal of marriage:

She felt him watching while she waited, gazing through the outspread scene, for words more in harmony than was this arch jocularity with the steady return of the strange new light within her that now streamed forth to join the blinding sunlight, so that she was isolated in a mist of light, far away from him and waiting for the sound of her name. (IV, 153)

In *Oberland,* where Miriam is "converted," there is a rich profusion of light on and in places and people, present and past. In *Dimple Hill,* the certainty of the presence of God within is the ultimate value of light imagistically, for the knowledge comes to Miriam as unearthly light, "the sly smile" of God. And the Quaker Roscorlas, symbols of life lived in constant acknowledgment of that presence, are "heaven-lit humanity." Even when Miriam has experienced the love emotion—intensely in a kiss, for example—the light appears to describe and evaluate the experience.[6] The range of experiences and feelings which may be illuminated by the presence of light in an image is great, but its central significance is constant: the enduring, ineffable reality within which is one's ultimate being and hence the means of knowing truth, beauty, goodness.

Is, then, the imagery of sensate consciousness divorced from the symbolic imagery of mystic consciousness? Distinct, but not separate, for the one becomes the means to express the other; the sharp perceptiveness characteristic of Miriam, extraordinary in itself, becomes meaningful beyond itself as the power of the intuitive perceptions from within is more and more sustained in the perspective of the superficial consciousness. The delight in nature becomes a delight for its "sacramental meanings"; the "shine on things" is as much the reality in them as the power of an illuminated consciousness to perceive it. The flowers in *Honeycomb* are no less real to Miriam than those in *Dimple Hill,* but these latter are newly real; therefore, perhaps, less emphatically sensuous in the style which renders their reality. Both, however, show the artist "perpetually illuminated" but "imprisoned" in the rhythm of the senses, conjoining the two in reporting the "glory" he sees.

Objectifying the states of mind which constitute the basic narrative, illuminating the quality of that mind as well as the environments on which it focuses, being sometimes expositor as well as describer, modulating to mirror the effects of passing time on a single perceiver—all these the imagery does in *Pilgrimage,* and we may therefore speak of it as the basic feature of Dorothy Richardson's style, one of her uses of language to deal with the problem of privacy and the problem of narrative in the stream-of-consciousness novel. But *Pilgrimage*, of course, is not just images. The images serve well the communication of a rhythm of the senses, but there is also a rhythm of thought, what Miriam once called a "spiritual metronome," which characterizes a mind. Creating a style to represent this in a stream-of-consciousness novel is another means of solving the problem of privacy.

3

The point of view that the phrase "stream of consciousness" when applied to fiction identifies a form of novel or a specific content, not a technique, has been convincingly stated.[7] We mentioned earlier in this chapter the three major techniques for rendering consciousness in fiction: interior monologue, internal analysis, and sensory impression. They are distinguished according to what level or area of consciousness is being exploited, and the relationship of the author to the contents of that area as they are narrated. Interior monologue allows a character to express his awarenesses in words and syntactical units proper to his mentality, with no evident author narrating. Functionally, it is a first-person formulation reproducing any area of consciousness in degrees close to or remote from speech formulation.[8] Internal analysis "tends to summarize the impressions of the character in the words of the author and consequently never strays from the region closest to directed thinking and rational control. It approaches the psychological domain which Freud calls the preconscious or foreconscious."[9] Sensory impression attempts to represent pure sensations and images from the area furthest from speech formulation. Combinations of these techniques are inevitable for the writer whose concern with consciousness is comprehensive.

In discussing the use of imagery we were aware of its significance in representing states of mind and modes of perception. It should be apparent now that imagery may be found in any of the three techniques we just described. For example, imagery used to represent pure sense impression is formally different from imagery integrated as commentary in a passage of reflective thought. It is primarily a syntactical difference. With a substantive to identify the object and modifiers to describe its peculiar sensuous effect on Miriam, Miss Richardson usually relies on the marks of ellipsis to accomplish the disjunct, non-verbalizing character of the passive mind receiving impressions:

The West End street . . . grey buildings rising on either side, angles sharp against the sky . . . softened angles of buildings against other buildings . . . high moulded angles soft as crumb, with deep undershadows . . . creepers fraying from balconies . . . strips of window blossoms across the buildings, scarlet, yellow, high up; a confusion of lavender and white pouching out along the dipping sill. . . (I, 416)

The connection of these phrases is psychological, not logical or grammatical. The marks of ellipsis suggest the linguistic discontinuity, but also a time lapse between phrase and phrase (or item and item) so that the discontinuity is chronological as well. In a succeeding passage the effect of this device is sharpened by contrast to the way Miriam's impressions of a display in one of the store windows along the West End street are presented. Her view focuses the items more nearly simultaneously than was possible for the street itself; hence, the use of commas and semicolons formally suggests the disjunct but temporally contiguous images:

. . . forests of hats; dresses shining against darkness, bright headless crumpling stalks; sly, silky, ominous furs; metals, cold and clanging, brandishing the light; close prickling fire of jewels. . . . (I, 417)

The phrasal unit of words is the same in both examples, but the punctuation achieves a space-time difference in the occurrence of the images. When the impressions register in Miriam's consciousness with a focusing thought to extend their significance beyond the sensuous, there is greater grammatical completeness:

Through the still, open-windowed brightness of the brown-green room, out into the naked blaze. Rocky dryness and sea freshness mingled in the huge air. The little baked pathway ribboning the level grass, disappearing round the angle of the enclosing edge, the perfect sharp edge, irises feathering along it, sharp green spikes and deep blue hoods of filmy blossom patterned against the paler misty blueness of the sea. Perfect. (III, 338)

The judgment expressed in the single word "perfect" provides the focus in which the descriptive items have been contemplated: their composition as picture to Miriam. The sensuous reality of the items is there but with conscious consideration of their further significance. The verbals grammatically connect the items in the scene—the pathway "ribboning" the grass, "disappearing" round the edge where the irises are "patterned" against the sky—and the connection parallels the mental composition of the items into a seaside view which Miriam judges perfect.

This last passage is not technically sensory impression as we have defined it, precisely because it does not reflect a passive mind receiving pure impressions. It is Miss Richardson's description of Miriam's perception. But it illustrates the difference between what has been called Miss Richardson's "early" and "later" manner. We observed earlier that there is a different disposition of the accesses to Miriam's mind in the early and later volumes, and that it is possible to account for it partly in terms of the later Miriam. Miriam is no less aware of the sensuous beauty of things as she grows older, but her typical perception then is less free, less spontaneously undifferentiated because of lack of thoughts and judgments. The almost ejaculatory directness of the West End street impressions is paralleled by the simple phrases that render them. The greater complexity of the seaside passage—equally concerned with sense impression—is, in contrast, accomplished by the relatively more complex expedient of verbal connectives. In either case, the style may be described as simple, functional rather than independently expressive. But the quality of the imagery allows an aesthetic satisfaction independent of the adequacy of the linguistic structures to imitate the mode of the impressions.

In the entire novel, there are relatively few passages of sensory impression with these simple stylistic devices. There are more which we can identify as interior monologue requiring a more complex flexibility of language. In *Pilgrimage* monologues usually occur when Miriam is alone. Sometimes there are brief shifts to monologue in the midst of conversations with others, or it is integrated in a passage of internal analysis. But any extended monologue represents solitary reverie. The least complicated instances of it depend simply on some means of showing the discontinuity of separate thoughts; there is no sequential thought, but by association, usually in memory, the pattern of the items can be understood. For example:

I *must* have been through there; it's the park. I don't remember. It isn't. It's waiting. One day I will go through. Les yeux gris, vont au paradis. Going along, along, the twilight hides your shabby clothes. They are not shabby. They are clothes you go along in, funny; jolly. Everything's here, any bit of anything, clear in your brain; you can look at it. What a terrific thing a person is; bigger than anything. How *funny* it is to be a person. You can never not have been a person. Bouleversement. It's a fait bouleversant. *Christ*-how-rummy. It's enough. Du, Heilige, rufe dein Kind zurück, ich habe genossen das irdische Glück; ich habe geliebt und gelebet. . . . Oh let the solid ground not fail beneath my feet, until I am quite quite sure. . . . Hallo, old Euston Road, beloved of my soul, my own country, my native heath. There'll still be a glimmer on the table when I light the lamp . . . how shall I write it down, the sound the little boy made as he carefully carried the milk jug? . . . (II, 256)

The explicit use of the first person pronoun leaves no doubt that Miss Richardson has withdrawn as narrator to let Miriam express herself. The almost completely full syntax of the sentences simply indicates that Miriam's mind is functioning at near speech-level, for she is talking to no one. The passage achieves the method of this area of consciousness by its lack of logical coherence, and by the use of words and phrases in the order and form of their occurrence to Miriam. There is slang (*Christ*-how-rummy); the bits of French and German rise from remembered readings to form associative links with her thoughts about "person." The few marks of ellipsis indicate breaks in time between part and part of Miriam's "stream"; the semicolons are shorter breaks.

In contrast to this rather intelligible and explicit monologue, there are those which occur when Miriam's mind is far more relaxed; the disorganization is apparent in the greater incoherence, the greater range of her thoughts, and a comparable disorganization in language. But notice that the statements, though sometimes merely a nexus of substantive and verb or a brief phrase, generally preserve the elementary intelligibility of communicable statement. Miriam considers a suggestion about the nature of "mind" read in a book; she does not sustain intensive thought about it; the statement simply drops, as it were, into a fairly relaxed mind and it is disposed of thus:

But if mind discovers that mind is unreliable, its conclusion is also unreliable. That's logic. . . . Barbara. All mind is unreliable. Man is mind, therefore man is unreliable. . . . Then it is useless to try and know anything . . . books go on . . . he has invented imagination. Images. Fabric. But he did not invent "dangerous." That is cheek. By this sin fell the angels. Perhaps he is a fallen angel. I was right when I told Eve I had sold my soul to the devil. . . . "Quite a good afterglow," and then wheeling alertly about to capture and restate some thread . . . and then later, finding you still looking. "M'yes"; a fine . . . fuliginous . . . *pink*. . . . God's had a strawberry ice for supper. . . . endless inexhaustible objections . . . a cold grim scientific world . . . Alma knew it. In that clear bright house with the satisfying furniture . . . now let's all make Buddhas. Let's see who can make the best Buddha . . . (II, 408)

The effect of discontinuity is achieved in the absence of overt links between parts of the reverie. Bits and fragments of thought and memory flow with uneven lapses of time indicated mechanically in the text. And yet there is a motif which the reader can perceive to organize the passage. Miriam has read the sentence, "There is a dangerous looseness in the fabric of our minds" in a book, and the "cheek" of it inspires the disconnected thoughts. The thought commentaries are linked as a series of reactions to the statement, but their forms are as various as they would have to be in nonspeech, relaxed verbalization. There are fully phrased statements of objection ("man is mind, therefore man is unreliable") ; allusion to a remembered Biblical occurrence that is relevant ("By that sin fell the angels") ; recollection of a statement heard in the past that is an instance of contrary evidence, offered to the reader as a dramatic image suggesting the power of illogic (the sky is "a fine fuliginous pink. God's had a strawberry ice for supper"). The obscure allusions to people (we know Alma and Eve, but not Barbara) enhance the privacy of the monologue without damaging its communication of sense.

As a pattern of style, such a passage breaks up conventional syntax and composition into fragments which give the illusion of the mind's processes under certain circumstances. Neither the decorative nor illuminative in prosodic devices (except the "pink" image, and it is incidentally illuminative) is used. The style's effectiveness depends on its realism and its power to communicate a meaning to the reader. The disorganization seems scarcely radical at all when we recall the ultimate disintegration and recasting even of the word in *Finnegans Wake.* The intention for Joyce and Miss Richardson was to imitate, as closely as language allows, the very process of mind. In Joyce's case, the closer the identity between the word and the contents of the profound unconscious, the less certain its power to communicate to the reader comprehensible perceptual significances. Miss Richardson's illusion is never so radical—and perhaps, therefore, never so actual—but it has the certain advantage of sustaining the reader's concentration on the perceptual significance of the contents of mind.

In these examples of monologue the first-person "I" replaces the "she" of Miss Richardson's general method. Even when the "I" is not stated, the first-person formulation is always assumed. But there are many passages in *Pilgrimage* which originate in the first person and show none of the other typical characteristics of monologue. The difference is in the area of consciousness represented. When Miriam is directing thought to a specific concern, her speech-level ideas are set off from Miss Richardson's third person description by their inclusion in quotation marks, much in the manner of James's later style:

Miriam flung off her outer things and faced herself in the mirror in her plain black hopsack dress. . . . "This dress is a nightmare in this room," she thought, puffing up her hair under her fringe-net with a hatpin. "Never mind, I mustn't think about it," she added hurriedly. (I, 354)

A few sentences further, the less completely formulated thoughts about the soap she is to use are presented as straight monologue, but without an "I":

The water hissed gently into the wide shallow basin, sending up a great cloud of comforting steam. Dare's soap . . . extraordinary. People like these being taken in by advertisements . . . awful stuff, full of free soda, *any* transparent soap is bad for the skin, must be, in the nature of things . . . makes your skin feel tight. Perhaps they only use it for their hands . . . advertisement will do anything, pater said . . . (I, 354)

When both the "I" and syntactical completeness are present, the style of the monologue can maintain the sense of privacy, a distinction from conventional first-person story-telling, by the manipulation of rhythm:

But I find my daily round at Wimpole Street dull. No, not dull; wrong in some way. I did not choose it; I was forced into it. I chose it; there was something there; but it has gone. If it had not gone, I should never have found other things. (III, 19)

The present tense of the verbs signifies the direct immediacy intended here; there is no auditor; Miriam is "talking" to herself. The tone of the language is conversational. Following her dependence on punctuation to suggest the tempo of a series of thought items, Miss Richardson uses the semicolon to effect an abrupt close of the short clauses constituting the thoughts, but not a complete stop, for the thoughts are sequential and closely successive in time. There is a staccato effect.

Rhythm in a style imitative of processes of mind would have to be natural, in the sense that the determinant of its pattern should be the expressive form assumed by the sentiments or impressions or reflections as they occur to an individual. Its measures are not, therefore, to be found in regularly metrical patterns, but in irregularly emphatic arrangement, slow or quick tempo, simple and direct or complex and devious movement. In the passage which we described as staccato in its rhythm, the statements are fairly uniform in length, and each statement is followed by a counterstatement in a forward movement of antitheses reflecting Miriam's indecisiveness about her job. The economy of words—generally a subject, a verb, an object in each part—allows the quick completion of statement, marked by a semicolon, and the immediate counterstatement following the continuum of the semicolon. With the exception of six, all the words are monosyllabic. The movement is rapid, uncomplicated, brief in the duration of its intervals between clause and clause; it is staccato rhythm suggesting a similar movement in the privacy of the mind thinking these thoughts.

In both sensory impression and interior monologue the rhythm is likely to be quick, sharp, uncomplicated, because of the single short line or phrase in the image or the syntactically truncated "expression." As we have seen, the marks of ellipsis help achieve a sense of tempo as do the other marks of punctuation. The pattern in sensory impression will be simple even when there are diverse lengths of phrase or varying arrangements of words for emphasis (as, for example, in the manner of attaching adjectives to a substantive in a phrasal image: "bright headless crumpling stalks" against the comma-paced "sly, silky, ominous furs"). It is in the full statements representing discursive, meditative thought that the rhythm is complex in proportion as the syntactical organization of the passage is complex, both suggesting through their order and rhythm the privacy of monologue.

As we read toward the end of *Pilgrimage,* this kind of monologue with an explicit "I" and complex grammatical involvement is more typical:

When he came in, and I saw him for the first time alone with one person, I thought I should discover the individual behind his unfailing sociability and felt a momentary deep interest in what he might turn out to be; what less and what more than his usual seeming. But although he said good morning quietly, and did not at once begin to talk, the way he took his place, and helped himself to toast and speared a pat of butter, was social. Even at that hour of a perfect, still, spring morning he was turned only towards humanity, keeping human lives in the room, the sight and sound and movement of them, and references to the past and references to the future. (IV, 274)

This incident does not occur in the narrative present; Miriam is recalling a friend in the past, and an incident involving him. She meditates on his quality in the growing gentleness of her own mood (in *Clear Horizon*). The language is hers: clear, almost completely free of animating figures. The sentence structure is complex, creating periodicity in the suspension of several clauses before a final meaning is clear. There are only three sentences in this long passage; each organizes separate aspects of Miriam's recollection of Lionel Cholmley. The second is typical. Miss Richardson identifies two facts about Cholmley in one compound dependent clause, suspending the two elements of the clause at the beginning of the sentence, and then concludes their relevance in three particulars, themselves suspended between the subject "way," for which it is an adjectival clause, and the predicate at the very end of the sentence, "was social." The tension between "although he said" and "was social" is sustained and slowly eased by the deliberate extension of the clause through parallel form and the repetition of "and" as a kind of continuant. The same technique is apparent in the latter part of the last sentence. The movement is slow, unhurried, compassing separate parts and suspending them for a final, summary resolution. It is the rhythm of contemplative thought.

But it is already apparent that in this passage we have

come very near to the predominant technique in *Pilgrimage*: internal analysis; the language here seems almost too much composed to represent unuttered thoughts. Were it not for the presence of "I" we might mistake it for internal analysis, for *Pilgrimage* for the most part shows Miriam's mind at alert, speech-level awareness. But the third-person perspective of analysis clearly shifts the responsibility of language to Miss Richardson, as she summarizes and analyzes Miriam's actions and thoughts. This does not mean that the style of the sensory impressions and interior monologues is not Miss Richardson's as surely as that of internal analysis; it is impossible that it should not be so. But the presence of the author summarizing or analyzing in the third person allows a freer development of his characteristic idiom than the more restrictive imitation necessary to sensory impression or monologue.

To generalize the characteristics of the style Miss Richardson developed for internal analysis, we may observe first that it is usually simple in diction, direct in expression. It is not colloquial generally, nor yet entirely "literary." This passage illustrates the style at its simplest and most direct:

She ate scarcely anything herself, keeping her attention free and always seeming to be waiting for someone to say something that was never said. Her broad-shouldered, curiously buoyant, heavy, lounging, ill-clad form, her thick white skin, her eyes like a grey-blue sea, her dark masses of fine hair had long been for Miriam the deepest nook in the meal-time gatherings—she rested there unafraid of anything the boarders might say or do. . . . Julia lounged easily there, controlling the atmosphere of the table. And the Pernes knew it unconsciously, they must know it; any English person would know it . . . though they talked about her untidiness and lack of purpose and application. Julia was a deep, deep nook, full of thorns. (I, 340)

It is obviously not an utterly simple style. Miriam is at dinner, contemplating her Irish co-worker, Julia Doyle. In a direct, straightforward orderliness, Miss Richardson describes what Miriam thinks as she watches Julia. But two characteristic features of anything Miss Richardson writes descriptively are apparent here: the dependence on a series of concrete adjectives to vivify a reference or the sense of something's physical presence; and a fondness for metaphor which establishes the quality of the nonphysical, "feeling" character of persons. Julia is a "deep, deep nook, full of thorns," a spiritual refuge, yet disturbing. Miss Richardson preserves, also characteristically, the sense of privacy in unuttered thought by manipulations of sentence structure. Here, the repetition of the verb "know" in several different tenses in a complex of independent clauses suggests the turning of a single idea in Miriam's mind till it satisfies her, and then (the ellipsis provides the pause) pursuing its further development.

The varieties of thought and feeling and action to be analyzed require many variations and elaborations of this simple form of Miss Richardson's style. Some of that variety will be apparent if we contrast the previous passage of analysis with this one, in which Miriam is described exulting in her first free days in London, and wanting to share her joy with someone. She thinks immediately of her old school friend Alma. Miss Richardson analyzes Miriam's excited recollection of Alma thus:

Walking home along the Upper Richmond Road; not lik-
ing to buy sweets; not enjoying anything to the full—always
afraid of her refinements; always in a way wanting to be like
her; wanting to share her mysterious knowledge of how things
were done in the world and the things one had to do to get
on in some clever world where people were doing things.
Never really wanting it, because the mere thought took the
beauty from the syringa and made it look sad. Never being
able to explain why one did not want to do reasonable clever
things in a clever brisk reasonable way; why one disliked the
way she went behaving up and down the Upper Richmond
Road, with her pretty neat brisk bustling sidling walk, keeping her secret with a sort of prickly brightness. The Upper
Richmond Road was heaven, pure heaven; smelling of syringa.
(II, 31)

The recollection of Miriam's mixed feelings about Alma is
a series of fragmentary impressions which arise and merge
quickly, one with the other. The grammatical form is
equivalent: a series of fragments parallel in form and
linked through their common participial beginnings, but
lacking a predicative solvent, just as the fragments of
memory are suspended in indecisiveness. The last statement is the only complete sentence, in a sense resolving
the prior uncertainties in the clear certainty of the place in
memory of the Upper Richmond Road with its relict of the
smell of syringa. The parallel, enumerative repetitions
secure a rhythm at once even and continuous. The repetition of the superlatives "never" and "always" heightens
the intensity associated with the sense of the passage.

The unpunctuated series of adjectives describing Alma's
walk as "pretty neat brisk bustling sidling" illustrates

again Miss Richardson's technique of concentrating qualitative modifiers before a substantive for a near-simultaneous effect. In an essay on punctuation, she advises:

It is a good plan, in the handling of phrases, to beware of pauses when appealing mainly to the eye, and to cherish them when appealing to reflection. With sequences of single words, and particularly of adjectives, when the values are concrete, reinforcing each other, accumulating without modification or contradiction upon a single object of sight, the comma is an obstruction. When the values are abstract, qualifying each other and appealing to reflection, or to vision, or to both vision and reflection at once, the comma is essential.[10]

At its best, Miss Richardson's style in internal analysis becomes quite complex in syntactic and rhythmic patterns. It is a style reflecting the sense and form of inspired meditation where emotion is tempered by careful thought, a tension producing passages like this one analyzing Miriam's discovery of the new beauty in old friends seen after her Oberland adventure:

Strange and delightful that this simple discovery should be so moving as to seem in itself enough as a result of foreign travel and should go on, while the general to and fro of remarks was assailing her attention, wrapping her in a happiness that thrilled through her voice which was now claiming her attention for its own quality grown strange; sounding the gentle south of England, the west country, too, perhaps, of her family's origin, and the large-gardened, uncrowded southwestern suburbs—as so often, before, she had heard it sound here in the alien north, where voices grated even at their gentlest and bore, for all occasions, a bared and cutting edge; but without recognition of its essentials beyond the flattering

assurance that she herself belonged to a superior, more cultivated way of being; the way of being that amongst the
Oberlanders had been all about her and of which at this
moment she was being aware as clearly as of the misty English
villas as it made, on her behalf, within the inflections of her
voice, statements clearer than any spoken words, enchanting
and delighting her as she was delighted and enchanted by the
people she loved, giving her a thrilling certainty as to the unseen future, shaming her into the knowledge that in her care
they were unjustifiable, that she had grown level with almost
none of them, and yet lending their quality to every word she
spoke. (IV, 138)

This single sentence is a compendium of the intricacies of
assertion and qualification, the interactions of perception
and memory, of sensation and thought and feeling, all
interwoven in an elaborate grammatical web of co-ordinate
and subordinate structures. The attention demanded to read
the passage fully is a gauge of its pace—slow, tortuous—
controlled by the long continuance of the sentence to its
complete stop: the pace of intensive contemplation. There
is a slow, uncertain rhythm begun with the emphatic initial
words "strange" and "delightful," which the following
clauses and phrases define, expand, illustrate in a gradually
falling movement, picked up and reasserted at every semicolon, then swinging further down toward the concluding
phrase. It is a fundamental pattern which may be more
clearly observed in a less intricate passage:

Toned up, in the midst of the fatigue left by the day, by
the interest of meeting them for the first time in the open,
she glanced at Hypo . . . (IV, 158)

Even more simple is:

Full, the rooms were now. (III, 488)

When Miriam begins writing literary reviews, she adopts a creed of basic style:

Repeating her laboriously acquired creed, "Beware of verbs 'to be' and 'to have' and of 'which'; begin article with adverb; pile up modifications in front of verb to avoid anti-climax; keep gist of sentence till end." (IV, 354)

It is, of course, Dorothy Richardson's basic creed, ensuring a rhythm as well as a properly climactic "meaning":

When he had gone, strolling back across the lawn, the leisurely, experienced owner of the Mill Farm, two miles away as the crow flies, but a bit further off by road, its woods and meadows and the many crooked stiles m'sister found so difficult to climb, and had disappeared beyond the larches screening the eastern end of the house and the stillness, broken only by the cooing of doves, once more enfolded her, its quality had changed. (IV, 449)

This is the typical style of the more complex internal analyses: sometimes less elaborate in the earlier volumes; sometimes more so in the later ones. It is a style suggesting the atmosphere of the contemplative mind, but it is also one consciously structured for its own expressive value in periodicity—its long suspensions of complete meaning in the sentence, and in cadence—its emphatic initial clause or phrase and its gradual "fall" to the emphatic final clause. An irregular, natural, but pleasing effect ensues.

This effect is chiefly secured through arrangement, tempo, and complexity of movement. There are other means of securing expressive value in the style. The importance of significant sound is central in Miss Richardson's

•

concern with single words or phrases. She tends easily to
alliteration in passages of internal analysis where, unlike
those of sensory impression, description is often subordinate but necessary. An impression of things is often integrated into an expository passage, and the evocation of
some precise quality of the thing is economically heightened
by the alliterative diction used to draw the reader's attention to it. And it sounds good in itself:

a coil of carefully crimped hair. (I, 399)
The sound of the sea drowned the present in the sense of seaside summers. (III, 93)
Here, with the many palms giving green light and life to the
little lounge. (IV, 173)

Alliteration is joined to metaphor in "Individual things
were straws on the stream of summer happiness." (II, 401)
Even when a clear-cut sensuous image or metaphor is not
present, the single word—the concrete adjective—often assumes the force of metaphor or the sensuous intensity of
Miss Richardson's imagery. If we call such qualifying
words (or sometimes phrases) epithets, we have a class of
stylistic devices including usages of this kind:

jerky little footsteps crunching along the gravel (I, 325)
low frowning voices. (II, 296)
"We used to burn Yule logs," flickered Mrs. Philps. (II,
304)
The new furniture peopled the room with clear reflections.
(III, 410)
As the thunder rolled, bumping and snarling away across the
sky. (III, 437)
Cook . . . had gone bonily away. (I, 247)

In the more restricted—and classical—sense, epithet becomes a descriptive phrase or word for people, summarizing their total impression on Miriam, as when she repeatedly thinks of a handsome Italian met in Switzerland as
"the oiled bronze" or of Miss Holland, her so-different
roommate in Flaxman Court, as "the chatelaine."

The approach to onomatopoeia in the first and fifth examples above is complete elsewhere, as in "waves flump-
ing" and "the crowd below moaned and crackled its
applause." In all these devices, as in the fully developed
images discussed earlier, Miss Richardson exhibits an
extraordinary sensitiveness to the physical reality of the
things she represents and an equal sensitiveness to the
power of words which convey the sense of things to
the reader. It is a poet's consciousness and often emerges as
poetic statement organizing separate sounds within words,
the words singly, or the words in context into an aesthetically organic utterance, as in this single line describing Mrs.
Corrie eating fish:

the fork in her thin little fingers plucked fitfully at the
papered fish. (I, 355)

The effectiveness of "plucked" is in a correspondence between its connotation of quick movement and the "quick"
sounds of the plosive "p" and the short vowel "u." All the
other words support the effect: short "i" in "thin little
fingers"; the brief fricative "f" followed by short "i" in
"fitfully" and "fish." The initial consonants produce a
subtle assonance; Mrs. Corrie's gesture and Miss Richardson's language merge as sense and sound. Poetic assonance,

heightening sound effect for its own sake (note also the familiar inverted syntax), occurs sometimes, as in:

Graceless she felt, ungrateful, and could not care. (IV, 141)

Another technique is Miss Richardson's use of oxymora to express what actually is thematic in *Pilgrimage:* the power to comprehend the disparate and contradictory as unity—and truth. At a sensuous level it is "the dark brilliance that filled the room." More abstract, conceptual is the "shapeless shapeliness" of thought. Even simple action can be regarded as gesture "with careful carelessness." And Miriam's perception of Emerson's quality as a "serenely tumultuous mind" is particularly striking.

Whether it is the imagery, the varied syntactical structures, the rhythms, or the single words and figures, the effect of Miss Richardson's style must be described generally as vivid; that is, enlivened—both as re-creating the sensuous reality of the life surrounding Miriam and the reality of her mental accommodation of it, and as engaging the reader's active imagination in comprehending—feeling—the life presented in the narrative.

It is thus an impressionistic style in the sense defined by Sir Herbert Read:

Essentially, an impressionistic style is one in which the logical structure appears to have been distorted in order to produce a direct correspondence with the writer's sensations. The projection of sensations or emotions into a given form is known in aesthetics as "empathy" (feeling into), and impressionism is the creation of means that facilitate this process. . . . An impressionist prose style is one that gives the illusion that the reader is participating in the events, scenes or actions described.[11]

And as impressionism, it is the ideal solvent for a narrative whose aim is to exploit mimetically the inner life of sensation, perception, and memory. The imitation is not entirely "true" for the reason that Auguste Bailly holds all impressionistic style to be limited: the horizontal character of words and phrases cannot really approximate the simultaneous, multi-leveled operations of consciousness.[12] But the illusion is effective; not perhaps as radically effective as the Molly Bloom monologue in *Ulysses*, but still it creates the atmosphere of consciousness.

For the style gets at the problem of privacy in a stream-of-consciousness novel by making a single resource of the conventions of prose and poetry, in the process creating the illusion of imitative faithfulness to the nature of consciousness, yet allowing communication of conceptual significances and meanings, and sustaining a dimension of aesthetic expressiveness significant in itself.

The identity of author and heroine in the narrative method of *Pilgrimage* and the clear fact of its autobiographical basis support, in her own case, Miss Richardson's insistence that any novel is a "signed self-portrait of the artist," his signature being his style, and the novel itself a "conducted tour" first and foremost into the personality of the artist, who reveals "whether directly or by implication, his tastes, his prejudices, and his philosophy. And thus it is the revealed personality of the writer that ultimately attracts or repels."[13] Style in a novel, then, is what attracted Miriam to Henry James, for his was "the art of beautifully elaborating the ornate alias." (III, 417) The same may be said of Dorothy Richardson's art, with justice.

CHAPTER V

The Open Box

ALL THAT WE HAVE said about the meaning, the structure and the style of *Pilgrimage* ultimately bears on its central fictional achievement: the development of a multifaceted characterization of Miriam Henderson. All of Miss Richardson's strategies of technique have been put to the service of defining and renewing Miriam's vitality in her many experiences. But Miriam, paramount as her depiction is, does not inhabit the novel in eerie isolation. It is certainly intentional that many parts of *Pilgrimage* do present Miriam as the single human figure reacting to the varied world about her. Miriam complained once to Hypo that "the torment of *all* novels is what is left out." It spoiled James and Conrad, otherwise favorites. And Turgenev:

Sad, shadowed sunlight, Turgenieff. Perfection. But enclosed, as all great novelists seem to be, in a world of people. People related only to each other. Human drama, in a resounding box. Or under a silent sky. (IV, 416)

Raskolnikov? "Boxed in, but differently. Travelling every moment deeper and deeper into darkness; but a strange Russian darkness; irradiated." (IV, 416)

We know how important the nonhuman is to Miriam's

(and Dorothy Richardson's) awareness of the fullness of life, and so we have the reason for her complaint about novels where people are related only to people. But the insistence on the nonhuman by no means diminishes the importance of human contacts in the novel. The extra-human is importantly there in *Pilgrimage,* but so is a rich and full background of auxiliary characters with whom Miriam has brief or extended, impersonal or intimate involvements. Miss Richardson has provided carefully against a resounding box, but the drama of people related to people is not ignored.

E. M. Forster would regard Miriam as a round character. It is also likely that he would regard the entire group of auxiliary characters in *Pilgrimage* as an instance of what he takes to be a basic accomplishment of the competent novelist—surpassing even the importance of "formulae" of point of view: "the proper mixture of characters."[1] Forster means by this a mixture of individuals sufficiently lively and varied, and complex in their relations one with the other, to parallel the impact of life on people, and the impact of a variety of people on the life the novelist describes. Flat and round are the kinds of character to be found in a proper mixture: the flat ones register a single idea or quality by which a reader at once recognizes them "emotionally" upon their re-entry into the narrative after their first appearance; the round ones are complex, promising surprise in their refusal to be anticipated as to the facet of themselves likely to be manifested at various turns of the narrative. And there are degrees between. The novelist's concern is to keep the flat character flat without relegating to him a function of mere type or caricature. Examples in

Pilgrimage are not hard to find. Of the characters with whom the reader becomes familiar by their appearance in many parts of the novel, many seem flat in Mr. Forster's sense. Mrs. Bailey, Miriam's landlady on and off for several years, is the embodiment of natural goodness and strength, to Miriam a "recognized centre" of instinctive wisdom. "Now, young lady" always alerts the reader to some expression of her quality. Sister Harriett, gay, untroubled by trouble, her irrepressible animation signaled in every utterance of "Mirry, old fing," is another. We could extend the list, but the fact of there being flat characters is not as cogent as the method of their presentation.

Pilgrimage is entirely bound to a single point of view, and Forster, in his concern for the proper mixing of characters, hints that preoccupation with point of view may be inimical to the writer's need "to bounce the reader into accepting what he says."[2] His meaning is not entirely clear, but his example from Dickens suggests that a novelist needs to maintain the privilege of moving the reader from character to character (and from point of view to point of view) to get the maximum perspective on the characters themselves and on their contribution to events. The stream-of-consciousness novel assumes a conception of character that is not static or horizontal because consciousness, which defines character, is not. Defining character from within, the stream-of-consciousness novelist is unavoidably involved in "point of view." It is certainly possible to "bounce" the reader from one character to another by shifting from one consciousness to another. Both *Ulysses* and *Mrs. Dalloway* are multipersonal in point of view: Joyce shifts it among Stephen, Bloom, and Molly; Mrs.

Woolf changes her focus occasionally from Clarissa Dalloway to Septimus Smith or others. But Dorothy Richardson foregoes this possibility by maintaining a unipersonal focus throughout *Pilgrimage.* When this structural discipline and the interior specification of character are combined, the conventional presentation of minor characters is considerably altered. In *Pilgrimage* all of them appear only as Miriam sees them. What, then, is characteristic of a flat character there, and what is his function? And how does a novelist bound by point of view as Miss Richardson is "bounce" the reader among characters for their maximum contribution to the novel's purposes?

Miriam sees people in the same way we have shown her to see—that is, to perceive—objects or natural scenes. The same attention to the expressive detail, whether physical or qualitative, which conveys a sense of a thing's reality, brings Miriam's impressions of people into convincing focus for the reader. No characterization is involved in this passage, but its illustration of Miriam's sensitiveness to people—their gestures, nuances of expression, discernible attitudes—strengthens our confidence in her point of view. Hypo, Alma, and Miriam are dining in a fashionable restaurant, and Miriam interrupts their conversation to comment on the voices of guests at nearby tables:

"All these manicured voices," she said quietly, leaning outwards to catch also Alma's ear, and collided with Hypo's voice and saw him drop his remark half-finished and swiftly turn a hopeful, investigating eye. Alma's laugh tinkled, abruptly accentuated; mirthless. An extinguisher. And whilst Hypo, accepting it, passed it on warmed and disarmed by a flattering, appreciative grin, Miriam saw, deep-drawn for her benefit on Alma's brow—as she turned to select an hors d'oeuvre, repeating her sound in order to assert her steward-ship of the conversation and keep silent during the instant required for improvising a fresh departure, the initiator of so unsuitable a topic—a pucker of disgust. (IV, 160)

Even many persons who appear once only, silently, in the range of Miriam's conscious eye, are reported with a peculiar immediacy and vitality. The single description becomes a miniature portrait, making precise something of the physical aspect of the person as well as something of his character—even if it is largely Miriam's speculation. Seeing a middle-aged couple in a hotel dining room, Miriam reads the husband as a man dominant and domi-neering:

Beyond him his wife, sitting rather eagerly forward, fair and plump, with features grown expressionless in their long service of holding back her thoughts, but, betraying their secret in a brow, creased faintly by straining upwards as if in perpetual incredulity of an ever-present spectacle, and be-come now the open page of the story the mouth and eyes were not allowed to tell. (IV, 41)

This is imagery in the service of characterization. The im-pression represents a point of view adequate to our de-mands to see, and to feel the independent reality of a char-acter, even one with only a moment's existence in the novel. The same is true with people whom Miriam sees longer and more intimately. Mrs. Corrie is a "tall graceful bird" with a "chalky, lispy voice that said little things and laughed at them and went on without waiting for an-swers." (I, 355) Similar imagistic descriptions of details

about Mrs. Corrie give the reader a rather clear view of
her appearance and type.

With characters who, like Mrs. Corrie, appear and reappear, it is Miriam's continual probing of their individuality which fills in more and more a picture of the person. For she tends to see them in more than one dimension,
to see them as the reader would like to see them for himself. Her extraordinary sensitivity and insight combine
with her inveterate analyzing and probing to communicate
rather definitely the character's "being" and the meaning
of his relationship to Miriam. Hypo Wilson, Mag and Jan,
Eleanor Dear, Amabel—all come alive to the reader partly
by Miriam's extensive and sensitive report of them. But it
is, after all, *her* report, not unmixed with judgment and
opinion which define the bias of Miriam's own mind and
thus threaten to get between the reader and a fair picture
of the auxiliary characters. This is particularly true of impressions of male characters, against whose typical mentality Miriam raises a strongly biased protest.

The corrective is within Miss Richardson's method, for
we are presented the characters themselves in scenic, dram-
atized events as well as through Miriam's pictured impressions of them. The scene presents an auxiliary
character in action and speech which reveal his particular
quality directly to the reader, who is able to consider both
Miriam and her associate without any intervening personality. The value of this direct method of character
presentation is particularly obvious in two scenes where
Hypo Wilson, who becomes a kind of whipping boy to
Miriam because his is, to her, so typically and so nearly
persuasive the masculine mind, is heard to develop his own

point of view in arguments with Miriam. In *Revolving Lights,* he and Miriam discuss at length her notions of the true distinction of the feminine genius.[3] In an extended scene in *Dawn's Left Hand,* there is a very revealing contrast in the qualities of their two minds as Miriam and Hypo consider one of her theories about speech.[4] Miriam's point of view is replaced by the reader's own, and perhaps the imbalance is corrected.

There are enough scenes with a variety of intellectual and emotional interest to make of the important auxiliary figures nearly round characterizations, or at least flat characterizations with potential complexity suggested. Miss Richardson depends on the spoken word in these scenes, for there is usually little significant physical action, and when there is, it is Miriam's description of it which we get. But the dialogue succeeds in catching the rhythms of individual speech and the representative vocabulary of the character presented. Michael's foreigner's English with its strange syntax, unusual emphases, and idiosyncratic preference for the superlative "most" to express any intensity; the sometimes adenoidal gentility of Eleanor Dear's soft, intimate, falsely emphatic manner, invariably apostrophizing her hearer with "de-er": "Lots of *influenchoo peopoo,* de-er"; or Mrs. Corrie's nervous, half-cockney jabbering at dinner: "Spinnick? Ah, nicey spinnick; you can leave us that, Stokes . . . Oh, you *must* have Burgundy—spin-spin and Burgundy; awful good; a thimble-full, half a glass; that's right"—these become gestures of the personality which Miss Richardson wants to define.

The method of characterizing these auxiliary figures is, after all, conventional in the sense that they are both described in the "abstract" and revealed in concrete speech and action. The difference is entirely in the point of view of the description—in this case consistently Miriam's, never the omniscient author's. The omniscient author's need to "bounce" the reader is accommodated in the direct presentation of these figures in scenes, though the area of such bouncing remains the area of Miriam's consciousness. Economy and immediacy, which "bouncing" apparently is intended to achieve, are not impaired by point of view as Forster fears, but rather are heightened by it in *Pilgrimage*. The bouncing is itself economized by the point of view, its area limited to the focus wherein it can be relevant.

It seems too that the characters who reappear time and again tend to take on roundness in the sense that their surface is "fleshed" out; we perceive more and more of the apparent character of Hypo or Amabel or Densley each time they appear. But it is a penetration in one direction; the characters seem round because a single, dominant impression of them is expanded or embroidered; the exterior impression has a single center but admits variations in its repetition. This suggests that in a stream-of-consciousness novel the round character is one the "original contents" of whose mind are exploited depthwise as the evidence of his identity; the flat character, however fleshed out, is one seen from outside himself, to be understood and judged merely by the social manifestations of himself in gesture, opinion, accent. In a conventional narrative, we distinguish flat characters by the single quality or gesture they invariably exhibit; in the stream-of-consciousness novel it is perhaps the restriction

to exterior view which generally distinguishes them. Septimus Smith in *Mrs. Dalloway* is not a flat character though
he is subordinate to Clarissa Dalloway; he is seen from
within and without, and tends thus to the real complexity
of the round character as the stream-of-consciousness
novelist must conceive it. But Amabel in *Pilgrimage* is
flat; her seeming roundness is but theme and variation on
a dominant external impression.

Once presented, the auxiliary characters in *Pilgrimage*
assume a function which gives them an individualized
reality—they are not stereotypes or abstractions with hands
and feet—and also a meaning which Miriam and the
reader alike perceive. They are fundamentally representa-
tives of types of personality, varieties of belief, and modes
of thinking usually in contrast to Miriam's own, even as
they exhibit a convincing individuality. Michael Shatov
believes the reality of the race is greater than that of the
individual; he is skeptical of the subjective; he is loyal
to scientific realism and political revolution; yet he is
gentle, humane, intensely emotional about and protective
of his spiritual relationships with people—especially his
eventual love for Miriam. Fellow roomers at Mrs. Bailey's,
fellow devotees of intellectual exchange—between persons, at lectures, in books—and for a time nearly married,
Miriam and Shatov are provided a natural, varied complex
of relationships. These relationships are entirely human-
ized, individualized, but it is as if Miss Richardson has
embodied two opposed points of view in the two figures.
The sustained contrast (Michael keeps appearing through
the very last pages) is equally effective in illuminating
Miss Richardson's point of view, through Miriam, and a

view which it must repudiate to justify itself; hence, Miriam's rejection of Michael's proposal of marriage because of the incompatibility of their life views.

During her greatest intimacy with Michael, Miriam is also shown in close, contrasting relationship to Mr. Hancock, one of the dentists for whom she works and about whom she has sympathetic and critical feelings. He "liked and disliked without understanding the curious differences between people—did not know why they were different—they put him off or did not put him off and he was just." (II, 53) He was of the world of people with "culture and refinement," dedicated to the sufficiency of science: "always looking out at something with gentle intelligence or keen intelligence . . . never really aware of anything behind or around them because of the wonders of science." (II, 102) And, symptom to Miriam of the benign blindness of his social perspective, Hancock is duped into admiration of "feminine" women, symbols of deliberate trickery in social method. As with Michael, she is attracted to and repelled by Hancock; the two men are themselves very different, but each bears a true mark of some aspect of that maleness which is offensive to Miriam and, thematically, central to the novel. They become individualized but symbolic parts of an ideological whole in *Pilgrimage:* the composite image of blind, complacent masculine intelligence and attitudes.

The figures of Michael and Hancock blend subtly into Hypo Wilson and Dr. Densley, themselves distinct individuals but continuing the masculine roles of Michael and Hancock into the later parts of *Pilgrimage,* where Michael is less and less with Miriam and Hancock has married, and thus is out of Miriam's concern except as her employer. Hypo is brilliant, talented, a literary savant, but barely tolerant of Miriam's subjective preoccupations, and possessed of what she thinks are narrow, constricting scientific formulae for comprehending life: a Lycurgan enthusiast, a devotee of the "new" psychological and philosophical realism, a cocky skeptic.

He was two people. A man achieving, becoming, driving forward to unpredictable becomings, delighting in the process, devoting himself, compelling himself, whom so frankly he criticized and so genuinely deplored, to a ceaseless becoming, ceaseless assimilating of anything that promised to serve the interests of a ceaseless becoming for life as he saw it. And also a man seeming uncreated, without any existence worth the name. (IV, 220)

His stability was the imposition of intellect on the inchoate life in which he submerged himself; and he was satisfied that that was *being*. Herein lies the point of contrast and conflict on which the many relationships between Hypo and Miriam turn and assume their drama: intellectual combatants, disagreeing socialists, lovers, the scientific realist and the romantic mystic. Hypo represents the pre-eminent masculine consciousness—and a charming man—a doughty opponent for Miriam to overcome in her pursuit of recognition for the reality of the feminine consciousness. Dr. Densley, like his earlier counterpart, is the obverse side of the same coin. Hancock's kind gentleness is also Densley's "secret life of faith in humankind, his shining love." He is genuinely social, though it means sometimes that he "rushed thoughtlessly through readymade evolutions." Undiscriminating but good, "bright strangeness rooted in an unexamined sameness," only charitably interested in ideas:

"But ideas, my dear girl, are not the greatest thing in the world. And they easily take one too far away from life." (III, 490)

A man almost man-womanly, but he too saw life superficially as process, never as complete being:

Faced alone, it appeared to him as bitterly sad, and the last disaster of an unhappy fate.

Faced in groups as he knew it best, it showed in his eyes only as material for comedy. . . . In life itself, the bare fact of life, there seemed for him to be no splendour. (III, 477)

Richard Roscorla appears briefly in *Dimple Hill* as nearly man-womanly: sharing the deep stillness of life within, alive to its spirit, turning outward in social honesty, living intimately with field and sky; the best of Michael and Hancock and Hypo and Densley refined under the Quaker condemnation of their masculine hypocrisy and blindness. And yet not *the* man; his is the technique of life that is being, but still a technique comprehending only the elemental life of farm and family.

The abstraction "masculine" has become successive men in *Pilgrimage,* each in direct involvement with Miriam and thus functional as indirect commentaries on their represented qualities and hers. Miriam develops, changes, and the succession of male characters achieves a corroborating testimony to her changes by becoming, each in turn, a new measure of the intellectual and emotional life the novel describes. After Michael has asked Miriam to marry him, he feels bound to confess his unchaste past, expects and gets a curious reaction from Miriam who is "shocked" but immediately upbraids herself, feigning indifference. But with Hypo Miriam willingly and freely is a mistress. The change is its own commentary; the men involved are its measure as well as its participants.

There are other, less prominent male characters whose function is similar, though perhaps almost mechanical. For example, "Mr. Grove" interests Miriam briefly as a possible beau when he attends her sisters' wedding in *Honeycomb*. After her first year in London, Mr. Grove turns up suddenly to call, and Miriam's reaction to the unchanged Mr. Grove reflects her own rather marked change. Similarly, in *Oberland* Miriam confronts the two Cambridge "men," Vereker and Eaden, on whom one might expect her scathing denunciation to fall. But Oberland has chastened her, and a remarkable gauge of the change is her calm, tentative discussion of socialism with the rich, plantation-owning Eaden.

The great number, and perhaps the greater independent interest, of female auxiliary characters extends the function of providing contrasts to Miriam. Mrs. Corrie—the shallow, brittle, self-satisfied, but "charming" woman of wealth; Selina Holland the "gentlewoman," her strongest word of contempt "unspeakable," dedicated to "high ends, any kind of high end," possessed of "vicarage humour," and who Miriam knew would want to "run the parish, choose the music, edit the vicar's mind, lecture the parishioners"; and the anonymous procession of "charming" girls, wives of professionals, feminists (suffragette variety), and masculinely intellectual women who move in and out of the narrative—all enliven the novel

with an interest of their own but ultimately provide means
of revealing significant contacts for Miriam and focuses
for her critical assertions against the false or dangerous
or misguided ways of life they represent to her.

With some of the more prominent female characters,
we see extensions of Miriam's own self. The Brooms,
friends from Wordsworth House days in *Backwater,* are
constant symbols to her of the good in English middle-
class life, a life that is a part of her own heritage from
which she cannot, and does not want entirely to, escape.
Their significance in this respect is apparent in Miriam's
return again and again to them with renewed satisfaction.
Mag and Jan, free and independent in London like herself, emancipated from convention, draw out a side of
Miriam's character unseen in her other associations: witty
good humour; relaxation into the spirited mimicry and
buffoonery which often characterize sessions of the three
young girls as they sit, smoke, wisecrack and otherwise
profane the current ideal of young British womanhood.
With them Miriam reveals a dimension of her own personality which is duplicated in the single aspect the reader
gets of the other two girls.

With Eleanor Dear, the situation is different. Seen
objectively, Eleanor is an unconscionable schemer, using
people shockingly for small and large gains. But she is
unoffensive, almost ludicrous, so unmalicious and des-
perate is her scheming merely to live free of the destitution to which her broken health drives her. She elicits
sympathy; underneath her surface presumptions with the
people she manipulates is an instinctive faith in their
ultimate capacity to absorb her need. And Miriam sees

this; realizes it as a projection, admittedly questionable, even perverse, of her own optimistic acceptance of the fact of life shorn of the uncertainties of right and wrong in human conduct. Miriam reflects:

To call Eleanor an adventuress does not describe her. You can only describe her by the original contents of her mind. Her own images; what she sees and thinks. She was an adventuress by the force of her ideals. Like Louise going on the street without telling her young man so that he would not have to pay for her trousseau. (III, 285)

Eleanor thus becomes a symbol of the life Miriam tries to reconcile throughout the novel. Eleanor is appearance and reality to Miriam; the drama of their relationship continues the drama of Miriam's to-and-fro quest for the reality beneath the surface of things.

Mag and Jan, on one of Miriam's visits, seem something less than pleased with her. Their usual jokes about "the Henderson" are rather more like ominous criticism. Miriam distresses them with her increasing seriousness, her tense intellectual miseries. During the visit they "sat far away, seemed to be more than ever enclosed in their attitude of tolerant amusement at her doings"; they say almost disapprovingly: "You will lose your colour, my child, and get protuberances on your brow." Miriam's change is again marked by essentially unchanging characters. Mag and Jan remain Miriam's friends, but appear less frequently in the later volumes. Amabel reorientates the reader to the Harriett-Mag-Jan cycle of Miriam's alter egos. Amabel is French, entirely feminine in Miriam's sense, happily aware of the incongruities of life and in perfect command of them; a Lycurgan and suffragette but

persistently undeluded by the limitations of either movement; incorrigibly gay and disrespectful to masculine
systems or conventions; she is the essential, eternal woman
Miriam herself, differently constituted, might have been.

The "life" quality Miss Richardson desired for *Pilgrimage* demanded as many and as varied a cast of characters
as we find there. Horace Gregory reads *Pilgrimage* as a
"true and humanistic comedy"; Miriam Henderson as
"the voice, the eye, the presence of a human personality,
a figure who appears as the chorus or property woman in
Miss Richardson's *Comédie Humaine* of English-speaking
Europe."[5] There emerges for him a set of critical views—
moral, social, political—which remind him of Dr. John-
son's "vigorous radical-Toryism." The great company
of minor figures in *Pilgrimage* are important singly and
together as objects and means of this criticism.

The searching critical accent within each incident presented and on each character depicted is inescapable—
and often profoundly provocative; it is not to be denied.
But if this were not merely a single, incomplete value to
be discerned in the auxiliary figures, the human relations
in *Pilgrimage* would be, in Miss Richardson's view, drama
in a resounding box. *Pilgrimage* achieves the illusion of inclusive life as experienced by an unusually perceptive
woman. And although the drama—if we will, the critical
drama—of human relationships is essential to that illusion,
it is not all of it. There are also the sea, the gardens, the
ineffable "feeling" in solitary contemplation, the voices
heard and unheard in memory—the list is long and runs
even to the sounds of closing doors. Together, they are
all caught up in the sensibility which feels them, and

under its power to apprehend the transcendant real they assume their ultimate value, which is not finally radical-Tory nor Fabian socialist nor sociologically Darwinian. It is, to Miriam Henderson and Dorothy Richardson, their degrees of nearness to or distance from the spiritual ideal defined to the mystic-artist as his intuitive access to transcendent or archetypal truth and beauty and goodness uncluttered by the exigencies of systems and creeds, dogmas and prejudices.

The critical faculty at work on the human drama of many characters in *Pilgrimage* is Miss Richardson's vision searching for answering glances in the vast complexity of life; the variety of the characters and their relationships to Miriam, the focus of that vision, are Miss Richardson's means of "bouncing" the reader into accepting what her vision bids her say. For that purpose, they are a proper mixture.

CHAPTER VI

Coda

SOME CRITICS have damned Dorothy M. Richardson's *Pilgrimage* for various reasons; other critics have praised it for various other reasons. Among detractors and enthusiasts alike there has been uncertainty about the precise character of the thing judged, about how *Pilgrimage* exists as a work of literary art. The analyses which this study offers as a reading of Miss Richardson's work have sought to establish precisely what *Pilgrimage* is as a novel and how it coheres aesthetically as an image of life. If these analyses of its meaning, structure, and style are a just description of *Pilgrimage,* we may conclude that it has integrity and coherence as a literary work of art, and that its character as such need not be uncertain to the reader who would approach it for its own sake, or to the critic who would judge its value as art.

Her novel was begun as an attempt to provide a "feminine" equivalent to the realism current in the English novel in 1911-13. We are correct in relating this motive to a larger movement of reaction against the exteriority of naturalist and realist fiction, or against a positivist philosophy and aesthetic. But the feminine equivalent turns out to be more than an idealist reconstruction in philosophy and a shift to inner experiences for the material of fiction; both of these commitments, shared with other writers of her generation, are absorbed in Miss Richardson's experimental subject: a woman's quest for a sense of her own real identity in a distinctively feminine consciousness of life. Creating a form adequate for the development of that subject collaterally produced technical innovations which in 1911-13 were new. Of course, by 1938, these were scarcely experimental. By then, Proust's similar reconstruction of a personal past had been complete many years; Joyce had achieved an almost exhaustive development of the subjective method in *Ulysses;* and Mrs. Woolf had created her own distinctive dimension in stream-of-consciousness fiction with *Mrs. Dalloway, To the Lighthouse,* and *The Waves.* But the thematic motifs and the method of *Pointed Roofs* were sustained and amplified with unwavering certainty during this maturation of psychological fiction; the original intent in 1911-13 remained Miss Richardson's objective for more than twenty-five years. And that objective was primarily to experiment in communicating the unique quality of a feminine view of life. It is to the accomplishment of this aim that we should refer when speaking of *Pilgrimage,* in its complete form, as an experimental novel.

Miss Richardson's technique itself was, of course, experimental when she published her first chapter in 1915. It bridges the accomplishment of the later Henry James and the fully exploited subjective method of James Joyce. Miss Richardson assimilated James's point-of-view principle and something of his style, but she went beyond James's restriction to subtle analyses of subtle human problems. *Pilgrimage* ranges far more widely—and on purpose, more loosely—than James's novels did, and it pioneers a greater psychological depth within characterization by exploring levels of consciousness omitted in James's preoccupation with conscious intelligence. Miss Richardson, like James, immerses the reader in a sensibility but, unlike James, she is content to exploit the quality of that sensibility for its own sake. She builds her narrative around the impressions coming out of that sensibility, not its objectification in action, and thus she avoids the kind of dramatic structure which is typical of James but which she thought unsuitable for her subject.

Richardson was doubtless aware of Conrad's and F. M. Ford's theories of impressionist fiction, and to those theories she is perhaps indebted. But the character of her own experiment is clearly original, moving her historically beyond James, Conrad, or Ford. Her impressionistic method involves linguistic and rhetorical innovations which were as bold in 1913 as her denial of plot and dramatic structure. Priority in thus revolutionizing the techniques of fiction entitles Miss Richardson to historical recognition as an experimentalist. By 1938 her innovations had been absorbed and extended, and had become conventions of subjective fiction. But it was she who had pioneered the development.

A careful reading of *Pilgrimage* also permits us to view it with greater clarity in its generic relations. The method of the novel places it in a class of fiction called psychological or stream-of-consciousness. The common assumptions and aims of Proust, Richardson, Joyce, and Woolf have been described specifically by Edel, Humphrey, and Friedman, but among these novelists there are distinctions which are perhaps more important than the similarities.

If we imagine Dorothy Richardson to have received "consciousness" from the carefully exploring hands of Henry James, and to have begun gently prying it apart without much regard to the concerns for which James explored, we can imagine further that James Joyce seized consciousness and stripped it to its unconscious center with rather more violence and authority. It is not altogether a matter of the greater genius capable of outreaching the lesser one where Joyce and Richardson are concerned, though we must grant the far more impressive ability to Joyce. It is a matter of beliefs and purposes as well. The common ground of all the subjectivists is a preoccupation with interior vision, an implicit denial of universally acceptable social values wherewith to interpret life, a common impulse to alter narrative conventions and language itself in order to communicate the newly significant private vision, and a conscious concern to exclude the author in order to achieve a direct presentation of life.

But in the matter of impersonality some profound differences between Richardson and Joyce assert themselves. Miss Richardson's impersonality is paradoxical; she is excluded from intervening in *Pilgrimage* because of her narrative method, but she is entirely present with her heroine who, as valuating center, is the pervasive intellectual point of view with which Miss Richardson identifies herself. In *Stephen Hero* and *A Portrait of the Artist as a Young Man*, Joyce achieves the same kind of "personal impersonality" through his autobiographical identification with Stephen Dedalus. This identification continues in *Ulysses,* but it is subordinate there. In *Ulysses* and *Finnegans Wake,* Joyce's impersonality is as complete as possible. There is no pervasive personal point of view which organizes and evaluates the life presented in the narrative, that is, no point of view with which the author identifies himself individually. The difference is apparent in the two authors' methods of meaning and structure: for her, meaning and structure are the discipline of the perceiving consciousness whose successive and changing impressions imply the novel's theme and organize its form; for him many meanings and an elaborate structure emerge in *Ulysses* through allusions, mythic parallels, analogies between widely different areas of experience and knowledge, and other devices. Critics have shown us the necessity of the reader's collaboration with Joyce in supplying (by knowing) the conceptual significances which organize Joyce's rich matter. *Pilgrimage* is far less ambitious than *Ulysses,* but its perceptual immediacy to the reader is self-contained.

Richardson's "illumination" and Joyce's "epiphany" define the authors' difference further. For her, the revelation is momentary and of the transcendent reality ultimately identical with God, an "opening" vouchsafed to the contemplative consciousness (more or less perpetually to the artist) and cognizable in phenomenal experience. For Joyce, the revelation is momentary and of the reality, the "whatness," of things themselves, the *claritas* of his aesthetic and thus the revelation to the artist of the identifying "radiance" of things which the artist observes and records but in which he does not participate mystically.[1] Epiphany becomes the basis of Joyce's method, the means of sustaining the impersonality of an author refined out of existence. The contrast is sharp with Richardson's necessary involvement of the person in the mystical illumination which, for the artist, is the "glory" under which he reports the testimony of the senses as personal vision of reality.

Virginia Woolf is also less personal than Dorothy Richardson. In her diary, Mrs. Woolf complained that the danger of psychological fiction "is the damned egotistical self; which ruins Joyce [she wrote this in 1920 with only *A Portrait of the Artist as a Young Man* in mind] and Richardson to my mind: is one pliant and rich enough to provide a wall for the book from oneself without its becoming, as in Joyce and Richardson, narrowing and restricting?"[2] She sought the "wall" of her own stream-of-consciousness books in multipersonal focuses of abstract themes presented with an exquisite sense of poetic form and texture. One agrees with David Daiches that *Mrs. Dalloway* "shows a brilliance and finesse in execution that no critic can forbear to admire" and (noting his special use of the word "minor") that *To the Lighthouse* is "minor fiction at its most triumphant."[3] But one also agrees when Daiches says that *Mrs. Dalloway* has "a crack that shows the light between form and substance."[4]

For Mrs. Woolf's genius was to create images of life twice refined. Her themes are time, personality, and death, abstractions regarded philosophically in relation to the human condition. Her method in turn seeks objective correlatives in individual sensibilities and in experiences which are often removed from the world of broad social reality. The life which *Mrs. Dalloway* and *The Waves* create is a life of emotional essence, admittedly effective through Mrs. Woolf's gift for rendering poetically a character's largely emotional response to the idea of death, his own being, or the vagaries of time. But it is the balance of her form and substance, the one superb and the other disquietingly rarefied, that invites comparison with Richardson. It is the point of Horace Gregory's speculation that Virginia Woolf's fiction—with the exception of *To the Lighthouse*—"compared with the writings of Dorothy Richardson, her English contemporary, is less durable and too often willful and shrill."[5] Miss Richardson's subject required her to show the heroine's apprehension of life at many levels and within both a private and a social matrix. There is the single refinement of Miss Richardson's view of these experiences through Miriam's unique perceptions and insights. Richardson may thus be engaged more directly with the problems of individual and corporate life than Woolf, though with the inevitable loss of Woolf's concentration on exquisite form. The difference between the two novelists may lie partly in their conceptions of the relation of art to life in fiction—one inclining to the "life" novel, and the other to the "art" novel. In any case, it is apparent that theirs are two rather different achievements within the stream-of-consciousness tradition.

Richardson seems nearer to Proust. Both explore chiefly their personal pasts as the matter of their novels. Both regard the superficial self and its social milieu as flux and change. Both arrive at a conception of the identity of the

"real self." And both achieve, through fictionalized auto-
biography, an account of their development as artists
which ends with the imminence of the novel the reader
has just completed.

But for Dorothy Richardson the real self is transempirical. An individual knows his real identity in moments of mystical illumination when, through sense
awareness of beauty or through contemplation of remembered beauty, he is aware of the presence of the transcendent real in himself and thus of his stable identity.
Proust believed the real self to be the consciousness of
unity and continuity which a person experiences when the
past is brought into the present by "spiritual" memory.
During the quasi-mystical ("privileged") moment of
their conjunction through the stimulus of a sense experience, the person realizes the continuity of the self and his
conquest of temporal flux. Proust's reading of life is therefore profoundly different from Richardson's. She once
remarked that she considered herself "a most ardent
Proustian without seeing life in Proustian terms."[6] She
thought Proust's undertaking to be "the reduction of
phenomena to their laws—the laws, that is to say, of
science and psychology to date as taught, for him, by
Huxley and by Bergson."[7] Proust's work shows a philosophical sophistication and originality that make us question whether he depended as entirely on Huxley and
Bergson as Richardson suggests. But whatever his sources
were, he did create a "law" which is both the essence of
his theme and the source of his method: the law of time.
There is no equivalent law in *Pilgrimage,* for Miss Richardson's undertaking was deliberately not to reduce ex-

perience to any particular conceptual system. She under-
took to present "life primarily," and saw her meaning
and structure in the capacity of the mystically illuminated
feminine consciousness to view the reality of life directly,
not through a conceptual law. *A la recherche du temps
perdu* and *Pilgrimage* therefore arrive at fundamentally
different readings of life, the one perhaps pessimistic and
the other optimistic, even though both novels exhibit a
surface similarity of conception and method.

The causative or motivating forces behind psychological
fiction are ultimately the forces behind all the major literary achievements of our time. Dorothy Richardson's work,
then, must be read as a part of the whole modern tendency
to seek, after what appeared to be a general collapse of
traditional beliefs and values, new certainties. Literary
historians define this tendency as the peculiar demand of
disruptive, divisive contemporary civilization on the intellectual commitments and artistic aims of writers. The
predominating desire of minds and sensibilities as various,
illustratively, as T. S. Eliot's, D. H. Lawrence's, and
Aldous Huxley's was to find again a stable meaning and
order in life. Eliot's belief in the persistent stability of
tradition in a philosophical-religious orientation of the
present to the past; Lawrence's plea for a new and radical
consciousness of man's total, unified being in "blood and
mind" as the beginning of his salvation; Huxley's early
"mastery" of life in sardonic intellectualism and his later
attraction to the quieter order of mysticism—these are
some major achievements in the modern writer's view of
his world.

Dorothy Richardson's neoromantic anarchism must be

viewed in relation to these significant insights and her adequacy judged as we judge theirs. She seems to stand apart, her novel almost *sui generis,* in her uncompromising commitment to the primacy of individual sensibility and to the greater reality (and sufficiency) of a feminine accommodation of experience. Unlike Joyce, who acknowledged the reality of the subjective and yet saw its further significance in the objective order of myth, Miss Richardson saw little order and hence little meaning beyond the individual's private adjustment to a mystically conceived order of transcendent being. Because it could meet the subjectivist demands of Virginia Woolf, the body of ideals we assume to have characterized Bloomsbury would seem superficially congenial to Dorothy Richardson. But one cannot find in the composite body of beliefs embraced by the famous friends in Bloomsbury, including the ethical theories of G. E. Moore and the aesthetic principles of Fry, Strachey, and Mrs. Woolf, a pattern for Dorothy Richardson's principles.[8]

She seems to speak for no major group, nor to be significantly close intellectually to other, better known writers in our time. And yet her early attempt to create an image of the age assures the historical importance of her work, even if we find her ultimate vision unsatisfying. And clearly her creative experiment in the techniques of fiction pioneered many of the achievements we associate with the modern novel. There is the added historical advantage that we may read *Pilgrimage* as a vast and specific reflection of the general upheaval which brought forth the best of Eliot or Joyce or Lawrence, an upheaval mirrored by a perceptive woman attempting in its midst a meaning and an aesthetic expression for its character.

We may read *Pilgrimage* as a provocative artistic achievement in itself, or consider more fully its historical and generic relations, or assess its value as a novel of the modern world. We may then come to understand why Ford Madox Ford thought that Dorothy M. Richardson, of all modern writers, is the most abominably unknown, and why Rebecca West thought *Pilgrimage* one of the real achievements of the time, a miracle of performance.

Notes

CHAPTER I

1. *Pointed Roofs* (1915); *Backwater* (1916); *Honeycomb* (1917); *The Tunnel* (1919); *Interim* (1919); *Deadlock* (1921); *Revolving Lights* (1923); *The Trap* (1925); *Oberland* (1927); *Dawn's Left Hand* (1931); *Clear Horizon* (1935); *Dimple Hill* (1938).
2. "The Novels of Dorothy Richardson," *The Egoist,* V (April, 1918), 57.
3. "Dorothy M. Richardson," *The New Republic,* XX (November, 1919), pt. II, 14.
4. "Imagism in Fiction," *The Nation,* CVI (1918), 656.
5. *The Spectator,* CXXII (1919), 331.
6. *Ibid.*, p. 330.
7. *The Saturday Review* (London), CXXII (1916), 138.
8. *Times Literary Supplement,* XVI (October 18, 1917), 506. Cf. reviews of *The Tunnel* in *The Nation,* CIX (1919), 721 and *Times Literary Supplement,* XVIII (February 13, 1919), 81.
9. Hereafter I will refer to the separate volumes as chapters. From the outset, Miss Richardson conceived of the entire sequence as one novel, and herself refers to the separately published volumes as chapters.
10. "The Break-up of the Novel," in *Discoveries* (London, 1924), pp. 140-41.
11. "The Work of Dorothy Richardson," *The Adelphi,* II (1924), 514.
12. *Dorothy M. Richardson* (London: Joiner and Steele, 1931), p. 23.

13. *The Twentieth Century Novel* (New York: Appleton-Century-Crofts, Inc., 1932), p. 393.

14. The following titles are, I believe, a fair selection of critiques and essays after 1932: Günther Kulemeyer, *Studien zur Psychologie im neuen englischen Roman: Dorothy Richardson und James Joyce* (Bottrop, 1933); Pelham Edgar, *The Art of the Novel* (New York: The Macmillan Co., 1933), pp. 320-28; R. A. Scott-James, "Quintessential Feminism," *London Mercury*, XXXIII (November-April, 1935-36), 201-03; Paul Rosenfeld, "The Inner Life," *Saturday Review of Literature*, XIX (December 10, 1938), 6; Horace Gregory, "Dorothy Richardson Reviewed," *Life and Letters To-day*, XXI (March, 1939), 36-43; Graham Greene, "The Saratoga Trunk," reprinted in *The Lost Childhood* (London: Eyre and Spottiswoode, 1951), pp. 84-86; Robert G. Kelly, "The Premises of Disorganization: A Study of Literary Form in Ezra Pound, T. S. Eliot, James Joyce, and Dorothy Richardson" (unpublished Ph.D. dissertation, Stanford University, 1952); and Walter Allen, *The English Novel* (New York: E. P. Dutton and Co., 1955), pp. 417-18.

15. *Authors Today and Yesterday*, ed. Stanley J. Kunitz (New York: H. W. Wilson Co., 1933), p. 562.

16. *Pilgrimage*, I, 9. When an abbreviation can be used clearly, subsequent references to *Pilgrimage* will indicate only the volume and page number in the Knopf edition (4 vols.; New York, 1938). Beginning in the second chapter of this study, where there will be frequent quotations from the text of the novel, references to volume and page will be placed immediately after the quotations rather than in a footnote.

17. *Ibid.*

18. *The Nation and The Athenaeum*, XXXIV (December 1, 1923), 343.

19. *Pilgrimage, loc. cit.*

20. *Ibid.*

21. "Adventure for Readers," *Life and Letters To-day*, XXII (July, 1939), 45-46.

22. "Novels," *Life and Letters* (and *The London Mercury*), LVI (March, 1948), 191.

23. "Adventure for Readers," p. 47.

24. See Leon Edel, *The Psychological Novel: 1900-1950* (New York: J. B. Lippincott Co., 1955), pp. 15-49, and Edmund Wilson, *Axel's Castle* (New York: Charles Scribner's Sons, 1931), pp. 1-25.
25. IV, 239.
26. I, 11.
27. *Ibid.*
28. In Mark Schorer's sense of "discovering, exploring, developing [the] subject, of conveying its meaning, and, finally, of evaluating it."
29. See Robert G. Kelly, *op. cit.;* Walter Allen, *The English Novel* (New York: E. P. Dutton and Co., 1955); and Melvin Friedman, *Stream of Consciousness: A Study in Literary Method* (New Haven: Yale University Press, 1955).

CHAPTER II

1. See Walter L. Myers, *The Later Realism* (Chicago: University of Chicago Press, 1927), p. 4.
2. See Gardner Murphy, *Personality: a Biosocial Approach to Origins and Structure* (New York: Harper and Brothers, 1947), p. 490.
3. Rufus M. Jones, *Social Law in the Spiritual World* (New York: George H. Doran Co., 1904), pp. 43-79; 97-161; 205-21.
4. *The Quakers Past and Present* (New York: Dodge Publishing Co., 1914).
5. Horace Gregory, "Dorothy Richardson Reviewed," *Life and Letters To-day,* XXI (March, 1939), 37.
6. Miss Richardson makes frequent use of special marks of ellipsis (see discussion in Chapter IV).
7. See McTaggart, *The Nature of Existence,* Vol. II, ed. C. D. Broad (Cambridge University Press, 1927), p. 479; also his "An Ontological Idealism," in *Philosophical Studies,* ed. S. V. Keeling (London: Edward Arnold and Co., 1934), pp. 273-94; and Rudolph Metz, *A Hundred Years of British Philosophy* (London: George Allen and Unwin, Ltd., 1938), pp. 378-79.

8. See "Mysticism," pp. 51-52, and "The Further Determination of the Absolute" in *Philosophical Studies*.

9. *The Varieties of Religious Experience*, Modern Library edition, pp. 418-19.

10. *Philosophical Studies*, p. 271.

11. Evelyn Underhill, *Mysticism: a Study in the Nature and Development of Man's Spiritual Consciousness*, Meridian Books edition (New York: The Noonday Press, 1955).

    Dorothy Richardson calls the Underhill study "the boldest and clearest sighted, the most comprehensive and lucid description of the mystic type, of his distinctive genius, his aim and method, his kinship with his fellows throughout the ages, the world-old record of his search and its justification. . . ." (*The Quakers Past and Present*, p. 91.)

12. *Ibid.*, p. 81.

13. *Ibid.*, pp. 8-33.

14. *Ibid.*, pp. 27-28.

15. *Ibid.*, pp. 30-33.

16. *Ibid.*, p. 81.

17. *Social Law in the Spiritual World*, pp. 132-38.

18. See Rufus M. Jones, "The God of Mystical Experience," in *Pathways to the Reality of God* (New York: Macmillan Co., 1931), pp. 22-44.

19. Underhill, *Mysticism*, p. 177.

20. See *Mysticism*, pp. 176-97.

21. *Ibid.*, p. 196.

22. *Ibid.*, pp. 195-97.

23. *Ibid.*, pp. 198-216.

24. *Ibid.*, pp. 232-65.

25. Discussing the attempt of Edward Grubb (*Authority and the Light Within*) to interpret the central Quaker beliefs and doctrines in terms of the "new thought," Miss Richardson reaches a conclusion which is the substance of Miriam's judgment of Emerson: "He leaves us with the 'notional' God of transcendental idealism, who is just as far off as the corresponding matter-and-force God of consistent materialism." (*The Quakers Past and Present*, pp. 88-89. Cf. James, *The Varieties of Religious Experience*, p. 32: "Modern transcendental idealism, Emersonianism, . . . seems to let God evapo-

rate into abstract ideality. Not a deity *in concreto,* not a
superhuman person, but the immanent divinity in things, the
essentially spiritual structure of the universe, is the object of
the transcendentalist cult.")
26. *Mysticism,* p. 243.
27. "The God of Mystical Experience," pp. 22-23.
28. *Supra,* p. 10.
29. *The Quakers Past and Present,* p. 23.
30. Dorothy M. Richardson, "Leadership in Marriage," *The New
    Adelphi,* II (June-August, 1929), 347-48.
31. *Ibid.,* p. 346.

CHAPTER III

1. *The Quakers Past and Present,* pp. 33-34.
2. See Dorothy M. Richardson, "Beginnings: A Brief Sketch,"
   in *Ten Contemporaries: Notes Toward Their Definitive
   Bibliography,* ed. John Gawsworth (London: Joiner and
   Steele Ltd., 1933), pp. 195-98; her "Journey to Paradise,"
   Fortnightly Review, CXXIII (1928), 407-14; and *Authors
   Today and Yesterday,* ed. Stanley J. Kunitz, p. 562.
       In his own autobiography, H. G. Wells acknowledged
   that Hypo Wilson is a portrait based on himself. Amy
   Catherine Robbins, Dorothy Richardson's girlhood friend
   and later Mrs. Wells, is lovingly drawn as Alma Wilson.
   But lest we are tempted to read *Pilgrimage* as a novel entirely *à clef,* it is well to note the opinion of John Cowper
   Powys, another friend, who insisted that Dorothy Richardson
   as a person was rather unlike Miriam Henderson in several
   important respects, and that the game of guessing "who is
   who" in *Pilgrimage* is fruitless.
3. *Pilgrimage,* IV, 524-25; I, 10.
4. *The Quakers Past and Present,* p. 34.
5. "Adventure for Readers," p. 45.
6. *The Structure of the Novel* (London: The Hogarth Press,
   1928).
7. *Ibid.,* pp. 62-63.
8. *Ibid.,* pp. 94-95.
9. *Ibid.,* pp. 97-98.

10. Robert G. Kelly, "The Strange Philosophy of Dorothy M. Richardson," *Pacific Spectator*, VIII (1954), 78.
11. I have relied here on Hans Meyerhoff's *Time in Literature* (Berkeley and Los Angeles: University of California Press, 1955), pp. 11-26.
12. *The Craft of Fiction* (New York: Peter Smith, 1947), p. 69.
13. *Novels and Novelists* (London: Constable and Co., Ltd., 1930), p. 140.
14. A. A. Mendilow, *Time and the Novel* (London: Peter Nevill, 1952), p. 152.
15. *Ibid.*
16. The entire chapter reads:
    "Another spring vanished. . . .
    "A sheet of crocuses singing along the grass alley. White, under trees still bare. Crocuses dotting the open grass with June gold. . . .
    "Suddenly a mist of green on the trees, as quiet as thought. Small leaves in broad daylight, magic reality, silent at midday amidst the noise of traffic.
    "Then full spring for three days. Holding life still, when the dawn mists drew off the sea and garden and revealed their colour.
    "Every one had loved it, independent of other loves. Become for a while single. Wanting and trying and failing to utter its beauty. Every one had had those moments of reality in forgetfulness. Quickly passing. Growing afterwards longer than other moments, spreading out over the whole season; representing it in memory." (III, 498)
17. *Pilgrimage,* Foreword, I, 10.
18. "Adventure for Readers," pp. 47-51.

CHAPTER IV

1. *Stream of Consciousness in the Modern Novel* (Berkeley and Los Angeles: University of California Press, 1954), pp. 62-64.
2. Notably, L. E. Bowling, "What is Stream of Consciousness Technique?" *Publications of the Modern Language Association,* LXV (1950), 337-45; Melvin J. Friedman, *Stream of*

Consciousness: A Study in Literary Method; and Leon Edel, *The Psychological Novel: 1900-1950.*

3. See Friedman, *op. cit.,* pp. 4-7.
4. Edel, *op. cit.,* p. 188.
5. Babette Deutsch, "Imagism in Fiction," *The Nation,* CVI (1918), 656. Cf. Friedman, *op. cit.,* p. 185.
6. See p. 57 and note 4, Chapter III.
7. See Humphrey, *op. cit.,* pp. 1-4, and Friedman, *op. cit.,* pp. 3-4.
8. See Friedman, *op. cit.,* pp. 4-5.
9. *Ibid.,* p. 5.
10. Dorothy Richardson, "About Punctuation," *The Adelphi,* I (April, 1924), 996.
11. *English Prose Style* (rev. ed., Boston: Beacon Press, 1952), pp. 154-55.
12. See quotation in Stuart Gilbert, *James Joyce's Ulysses* (rev. ed., New York: Vintage Books, 1955), pp. 14-16.
13. "Novels," *Life and Letters* (and *The London Mercury*), LVI (March, 1948), 190-91.

CHAPTER V

1. *Aspects of the Novel* (New York: Harcourt, Brace and Co., 1927), pp. 120-21.
2. *Ibid.,* p. 119.
3. III, 256-62.
4. IV, 161-66.
5. "Dorothy Richardson Reviewed," p. 37.

CHAPTER VI

1. See Irene Hendry, "Joyce's Epiphanies," in *Critiques and Essays on Modern Fiction,* ed. John W. Aldridge (New York: The Ronald Press, 1952), pp. 129-31.
2. *A Writer's Diary,* ed. Leonard Woolf (London: The Hogarth Press, 1953), p. 23.
3. *The Novel and the Modern World* (Chicago: University of Chicago Press, 1939), pp. 182-83.
4. *Ibid.,* p. 182.

5. "Reunion at Bloomsbury," review of Clive Bell's *Old Friends* (London, 1956), *New York Times,* Book Review Section, February 10, 1957, p. 7.

6. "Mr. Clive Bell's Proust," *The New Adelphi,* II (1928-29), 161.

7. *Ibid.*

8. See J. K. Johnstone, *The Bloomsbury Group* (New York: The Noonday Press, 1954).

Bibliography

Primary Sources

Selected Writings by Dorothy Miller Richardson

"About Punctuation," *The Adelphi*, I (1923-24), 990-96.
"Adventure for Readers," *Life and Letters To-day*, XXII (July, 1939), 45-52.
"Beginnings: A Brief Sketch," in *Ten Contemporaries: Notes Toward Their Definitive Bibliography* (second series), ed. John Gawsworth. London: Joiner and Steele Ltd., 1933.
"Continuous Performance," *Close-up*, I-X (1927-33).
"In the Garden," *Transatlantic Review*, II (August, 1924), 141-43.
John Austen and the Inseparables. London: William Jackson Ltd., 1930.
"Journey to Paradise," *Fortnightly Review*, CXXIII (1928), 407-14.
"Leadership in Marriage," *The New Adelphi*, II (1928-29), 345-48.
"Man Never Is. . . ," *The Adelphi* (new series), I (1930-31), 521-22.
"Mr. Clive Bell's Proust," *The New Adelphi*, II (1928-29), 160-62.
"A Note on George Fox," *The Adelphi*, II (1924), 148-50.
"Novels," *Life and Letters*, LVI (1948), 188-92.
Pilgrimage. 4 volumes. New York: Alfred A. Knopf, 1938.
"Portrait of an Evangelist," *The New Adelphi*, I (1928), 270-71.
The Quakers Past and Present. New York: Dodge Publishing Co., 1914.

"The Return of William Wordsworth," *The Adelphi* (new series), I (December, 1930), supplement, xvi-xix.

"The Status of Illustrative Art," *The Adelphi*, III (June, 1925), 54-57.

"Visitor" and "Visit," *Life and Letters*, XLVI (1945), 167-81.

"Work in Progress," *Life and Letters*, XLIX (April, 1946), 20-44.

Ibid., XLIX (May, 1946), 99-114.

Ibid., LI (November, 1946), 79-88.

"Yeats of Bloomsbury," *Life and Letters To-day*, XXI (April, 1939), 60-66.

Secondary Sources

Aldington, Richard. "The Approach to M. Marcel Proust," *Dial*, LXIX (1920), 341-46.

Allen, Walter. *The English Novel*. New York: E. P. Dutton and Co., 1955.

Anon. review of *Deadlock*, *The Spectator*, CXXVI (1921), 403.

Anon. review of *The Tunnel*, *The Spectator*, CXXII (1919), 330-31.

Auerbach, Erich. *Mimesis*, tr. Willard R. Trask. Princeton: Princeton University Press, 1953.

Beach, Joseph W. *The Twentieth Century Novel*. New York: Appleton-Century-Crofts, Inc., 1932.

Bentley, Phyllis. *Some Observations on the Art of Narrative*. London: Home and Van Thal, 1946.

Beresford, J. D. "The Future of the Novel," *London Bookman*, December, 1930.

Bourne, Randolph. "An Imagist Novel," *Dial*, LXIV-LXV (1918), 451.

Bowling, L. E. "What Is Stream of Consciousness Technique?" *Publications of the Modern Language Association*, LXV (1950), 337-45.

Brittain, Vera. *Lady into Woman*. New York: The Macmillan Co., 1953.

Brown, E. K. *Rhythm in the Novel*. Toronto: University of Toronto Press, 1950.

"Cagey Subconsciousness." Anon. review of *Pilgrimage*, *Time*, XXXII (December 5, 1938), 70.

Daiches, David. *The Novel and the Modern World.* Chicago: University of Chicago Press, 1939.

Deutsch, Babette. "Freedom and the Grace of God," *Dial,* LXVII (November 15, 1919), 441-42.

————. "Imagism in Fiction," *The Nation,* CVI (1918), 656.

Eagleson, Harvey. "Pedestal for Statue: The Novels of Dorothy M. Richardson," *Sewanee Review,* XLII (1934), 42-53.

Edel, Leon. *The Psychological Novel: 1900-1950.* New York: J. B. Lippincott Co., 1955.

————. "Dorothy M. Richardson, 1882-1957," *Modern Fiction Studies,* IV (1958), 165-68.

Edgar, Pelham. *The Art of the Novel.* New York: The Macmillan Co., 1933.

"Fiction of To-day." Anon. review of *Backwater, The Saturday Review* (London), CXXII (1916), 138.

Forster, E. M. *Aspects of the Novel.* New York: Harcourt, Brace and Co., 1927.

————. *The Development of English Prose Style between 1918 and 1939.* Glasgow: Jackson, Son and Co., 1945.

Frank, Joseph. "Spatial Form in the Modern Novel," in *Critiques and Essays on Modern Fiction,* ed. John W. Aldridge. New York: The Ronald Press, 1952, pp. 43-67.

Fraser, G. S. *The Modern Writer and His World.* London: Derek Verschoyle, 1953.

Friedman, Melvin. *Stream of Consciousness: A Study in Literary Method.* New Haven: Yale University Press, 1955.

Frierson, William. *The English Novel in Transition.* Norman: University of Oklahoma Press, 1942.

Greene, Graham. "The Saratoga Trunk," in *The Lost Childhood.* London: Eyre and Spottiswoode, 1951.

Gregory, Horace. "Dorothy Richardson Reviewed," *Life and Letters To-day,* XXI (March, 1939), 36-45.

————. "Reunion at Bloomsbury." Review of *Old Friends* by Clive Bell, *New York Times,* Book Review Section, February 10, 1957, p. 7.

Hendry, Irene. "Joyce's Epiphanies," in *Critiques and Essays on Modern Fiction,* ed. John W. Aldridge. New York: The Ronald Press, 1952, pp. 129-143.

Hoops, Reinald. *Der Einfluss der Psychoanalyse auf der englische Literatur.* Heidelberg: C. Winter, 1934.

Howe, Susanne. *Wilhelm Meister and His English Kinsmen.* New York: Columbia University Press, 1930.

Humphrey, Robert. *Stream of Consciousness in the Modern Novel.* Berkeley and Los Angeles: University of California Press, 1954.

Hunt, Una. Review of Deadlock, *The New Republic,* XXIX (1922), 313-14.

Hyde, Lawrence. "The Work of Dorothy Richardson," *The Adelphi,* II (1924), 508-17.

Isaacs, J. *An Assessment of Twentieth-Century Literature.* London: Secker and Warburg, 1951.

James, Henry. "The Art of Fiction," in *The Future of the Novel,* ed. Leon Edel. New York: Vintage Books, 1956, pp. 3-28.

James, William. *The Principles of Psychology.* 2 volumes. New York: Henry Holt and Co., 1890.

————. *The Varieties of Religious Experience.* Modern Library edition. New York: Random House, n.d.

Johnstone, J. K. *The Bloomsbury Group.* New York: The Noonday Press, 1954.

Jones, Rufus M. *The Inner Life.* New York: The Macmillan Co., 1916.

————. *New Studies in Mystical Religion.* New York: The Macmillan Co., 1928.

————. *Pathways to the Reality of God.* New York: The Macmillan Co., 1931.

————. *Social Law in the Spiritual World.* New York: George H. Doran Co., 1904.

————. *Spirit in Man.* Stanford: Stanford University Press, 1941.

————. *Studies in Mystical Religion.* London: Macmillan and Co., Ltd., 1909.

Kelly, Robert G. "The Premises of Disorganization: A Study of Literary Form in Ezra Pound, T. S. Eliot, James Joyce, and Dorothy Richardson." Unpublished Ph.D. dissertation, Stanford University, 1952.

————. "The Strange Philosophy of Dorothy M. Richardson," *Pacific Spectator,* VIII (1954), 76-82.

Kulemeyer, Günther. *Studien zur Psychologie im neuen englischen Roman: Dorothy Richardson und James Joyce.* Bottrop, 1933.

Kunitz, Stanley J. (ed.), *Authors Today and Yesterday.* New York: H. W. Wilson Co., 1933.

[————] "Dilly Tante Observes," *Wilson Bulletin for Librarians,* VI (December, 1931), 285.

———— and Haycraft, Howard. *Twentieth Century Authors.* New York: H. W. Wilson Co., 1942.

Lehmann, A. G. *The Symbolist Aesthetic in France.* Oxford: Basil Blackwell, 1950.

Lubbock, Percy. *The Craft of Fiction.* New York: Peter Smith, 1947.

Mansfield, Katherine. *Novels and Novelists,* ed. J. Middleton Murry. London: Constable and Co. Ltd., 1930.

McTaggart, J. McT. E. *The Nature of Existence.* Volume II. ed. C. D. Broad. Cambridge: Cambridge University Press, 1927.

————. *Philosophical Studies,* ed. S. V. Keeling. London: Edward Arnold and Co., 1934.

Mendilow, A. A. *Time and the Novel.* London: Peter Nevill, 1952.

Meyerhoff, Hans. *Time in Literature.* Berkeley and Los Angeles: University of California Press, 1955.

Millett, Fred B. *Contemporary British Literature.* New York: Harcourt, Brace and Co., 1948.

"Miss Dorothy M. Richardson." Obituary, London *Times,* June 18, 1957, p. 13.

Muir, Edwin. *The Structure of the Novel.* London: The Hogarth Press, 1928.

Murphy, Gardner. *Personality: A Biosocial Approach to Origins and Structure.* New York: Harper and Brothers, 1947.

Murry, J. Middleton. "The Break-up of the Novel," in *Discoveries.* London: W. Collins Sons and Co. Ltd., 1924.

————. "Metaphor," in *Countries of the Mind* (second series). London: Oxford University Press, 1931.

Myers, Walter L. *The Later Realism.* Chicago: University of Chicago Press, 1927.

Neumann, Erich. *Amor and Psyche: The Psychic Development of the Feminine,* tr. Ralph Manheim. Bollingen Series LIV. New York: Pantheon Books Inc., 1956.

"New Novels." Anon. review of *Honeycomb, Times Literary Supplement,* XVI (October 16, 1917), 506.

"New Novels: *Interim.*" Anon. review, *Times Literary Supplement,* XVIII (December 18, 1919), 766.

"The Novel in Disintegration," *Times Literary Supplement,* Special Autumn Number, August 28, 1953, p. xii.

O'Connor, William Van (ed.). *Forms of Modern Fiction.* Minneapolis: University of Minnesota Press, 1948.

P. L. "Books and Things," *The New Republic,* XXVI (1921), 267.

"Pilgrimage." Anon. review, *The Nation,* CIX (1919), 720-21.

Powys, John C. *Dorothy M. Richardson.* London: Joiner and Steele, 1931.

Priestley, J. B. "Revolving Lights," *The London Mercury,* VIII (1923), 208-10.

"Proust, Joyce, and Miss Richardson," *The Spectator,* CXXX (1923), 1084-85.

Read, Herbert. *English Prose Style.* Rev. ed. Boston: Beacon Press, 1952.

Rosenfeld, Paul. "The Inner Life," *Saturday Review of Literature,* XIX (December 10, 1938), 6.

Rourke, Constance. "Dorothy M. Richardson," *The New Republic,* XX (November 26, 1919), pt. II, 14.

Schorer, Mark. "Technique as Discovery," in *Critiques and Essays on Modern Fiction,* ed. John W. Aldridge. New York: The Ronald Press, 1952, pp. 67-83.

Scott, Evelyn. "A Contemporary of the Future," *Dial,* LXIX (1920), 353.

Scott-James, R. A. *Fifty Years of English Literature: 1900-1950.* London: Longmans, Green and Co., 1951.

————. "Quintessential Feminism," *London Mercury,* XXXIII (November-April, 1935-36), 201-03.

Sinclair, May. *The New Idealism.* London: Macmillan and Co. Ltd., 1922.

————. "The Novels of Dorothy Richardson," *The Egoist,* V (April, 1918), 57.

Stace, W. T. *Religion and the Modern Mind.* Philadelphia: J. B. Lippincott Co., 1952.

Swinnerton, Frank. *The Georgian Scene.* New York: Farrar and Rinehart, 1934.

Thorburn, John M. *Art and the Unconscious.* London: Kegan Paul, Trench, Trubner and Co. Ltd., 1925.

Tindall, W. Y. *Forces in Modern British Literature.* New York: Alfred A. Knopf. 1947.

"The Tunnel." Anon. review, *Times Literary Supplement*, XVIII (February 13, 1919), 81.

Underhill, Evelyn. *Mysticism: A Study in the Nature and Development of Man's Spiritual Consciousness.* Meridian Books edition. New York: The Noonday Press, 1955.

"Varnish." Anon. review, *The Nation and The Athenaeum*, XXIX (1921), 621-22.

Wellek, Rene, and Warren, Austin. *Theory of Literature.* New York: Harcourt, Brace and Co., 1949.

Wilson, Edmund. *Axel's Castle.* New York: Charles Scribner's Sons, 1931.

Woolf, Virginia. *The Common Reader.* New York: Harcourt, Brace and Co., 1925.

————. "Mr. Bennett and Mrs. Brown," *The Nation and The Athenaeum*, XXXIV (December 1, 1923), 342-43.

————. *A Writer's Diary,* ed. Leonard Woolf. London: The Hogarth Press, 1953.

ACKNOWLEDGMENTS

To Professors Warner Rice and Joe Lee Davis I am specially indebted: to Warner Rice for many kindnesses during several years, not the least of which was his active interest on behalf of this book; to Joe Lee Davis for introducing me to *Pilgrimage* and, with ideal counsel and encouragement, directing the dissertation from which this book developed.

Dorothy Foster prepared the typescript with intelligent care. Louella and Jeanne supported me when they could not have realized they did.

To all of them I gladly express my fullest gratitude.